Drive and Stroll

Berkshire

Les Maple

COUNTRYSIDE BOOKS
NEWBURY BERKSHIRE

First published 2006
© Les Maple 2006

COUNTRYSIDE BOOKS
3 Catherine Road
Newbury, Berkshire

To view our complete range of books
please visit us at
www.countrysidebooks.co.uk

ISBN 1 85306 952 3
EAN 978 1 85306 952 9

Cover picture of the River Thames
at Cookham
supplied by Derek Forss

Designed by Peter Davies, Nautilus Design
Typeset by Mac Style, Nafferton, E. Yorkshire
Produced through MRM Associates Ltd., Reading
Printed by Woolnough Bookbinding Ltd., Irthlingborough

Contents

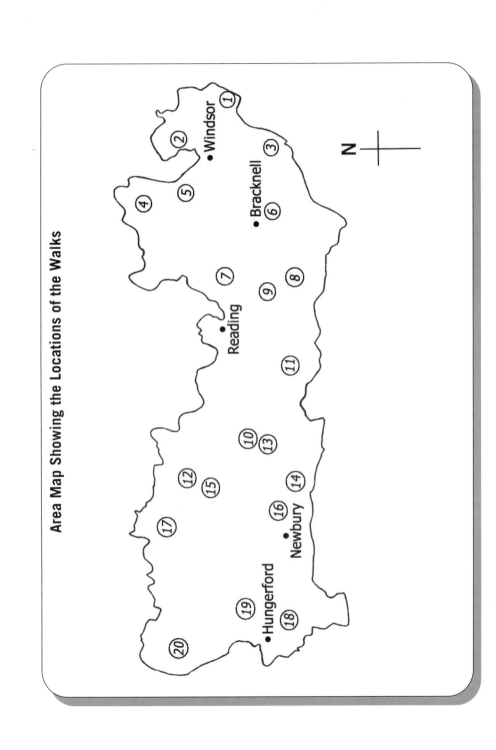

Area Map Showing the Locations of the Walks

Contents

PUBLISHER'S NOTE

We hope that you obtain considerable enjoyment from this book; great care has been taken in its preparation. Although at the time of publication all routes followed public rights of way or permitted paths, diversion orders can be made and permissions withdrawn

We cannot, of course, be held responsible for such diversion orders and any inaccuracies in the text which result from these or any other changes to the routes nor any damage which might result from walkers trespassing on private property. We are anxious, though, that all details covering the walks are kept up to date and would therefore welcome information from readers which would be relevant to future editions.

The simple sketch maps that accompany the walks in this book are based on notes made by the author whilst checking out the routes on the ground. They are designed to show you how to reach the start, to point out the main features of the overall circuit and they contain a progression of numbers that relate to the paragraphs of the text.

However, for the benefit of a proper map, we do recommend that you purchase the relevant Ordnance Survey sheet covering your walk. The Ordnance Survey maps are widely available, especially through booksellers and local newsagents.

Introduction

One of the best ways to see the countryside is to drive to a location, don a pair of walking boots, pack some waterproofs, just in case, and take a leisurely stroll, allowing yourself time to stop, look and perhaps take photographs. Royal Berkshire, although small compared to many of the other English counties, is steeped in history and packed with interest. Its rich and varied landscape contains open downland, commons, parks, rivers, wetlands, lakes and woodland.

Berkshire can be divided almost into two. In the rural west, the villages are more remote and further apart and it is here that we find the Lambourn and Berkshire downs and their connection with the training of racehorses. In the east, where housing and commercial development are more concentrated, it is thought that unspoilt pockets of peace and tranquillity are difficult to find, but I can assure you that they are definitely there.

Berkshire's 'Royal' title comes from its connections with Windsor Castle, which has been a royal residence since 1110 when Henry I set up court there. Near Wraysbury is the spot where, in 1215, King John affixed his seal to the Magna Carta, a document that has formed the basis of many constitutions, including that of the USA.

Several of the walks visit commons. One of the most well known, Greenham Common, has reverted to what it was prior to 1940, that of a large open space, with a rich variety of plants and associated fauna. Sites of Special Scientific Interest exist at Swinley Park and Englemere Pond and there is an interesting reedbed nature reserve at Thatcham.

There is a wide variety of pubs and inns to be found amongst the towns and villages and most provide snacks, lunches and/or evening meals. If you decide to park at an inn, please check with the landlord that he is happy for you to use the car park while you walk.

This collection of strolls is but a small sample of the many opportunities that Berkshire has to offer. I hope that the varied interests described here will entice you back for more, if only to revisit them at different times of the year to experience the glorious scenery in all its rich variety of mood, colour, and texture. To make the day complete, I have included at the end of each stroll a place of interest that is within easy reach of the start of the walk.

So, fill up your tank, lace up your boots, sharpen your appetite, and enjoy a stroll and, perhaps, visit a local attraction. Whatever your choice, have a pleasant day, and do remember the Country Code.

Les Maple

1 | Wraysbury

Wraysbury windmill

The Walk 4 miles ⏱ 2¹/₂ hours
Map OS Explorer 160 – Windsor, Weybridge & Bracknell (GR 004742)

How to get there

From junction 13 of the M25 take the B376 (signed to Wraysbury). As you enter the village of Wraysbury the B376 bends sharply to the left. 200 yards after this turning, turn right into The Green. **Parking:** Continue to the far end where there is a car park (free) on the right.

Drive and Stroll

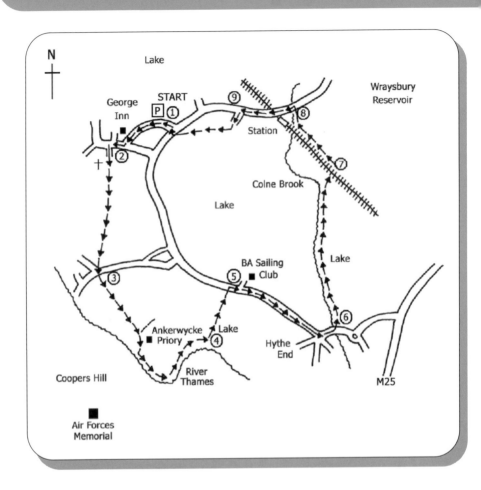

Introduction

The history of Wraysbury, or Wyrardisbury, dates back to Saxon times and possibly even earlier. With the River Thames encircling it to the south and west, and the River Colne to the east, the village has had its fair share of flooding in the past. This level walk takes in part of the village, passing the windmill and St Andrew's church, before heading towards the Thames and the Ankerwycke Estate where, near to the ruins of an old nunnery, stands an ancient yew tree where, it is said, a royal clandestine meeting once took place. Nearby, but not seen, is the island where King John set his seal on the Magna Carta.

The George Inn

Originally built during the 17th century, the inn has been subsequently enlarged. Beers on offer included Greene King IPA and Courage Best. Food includes cod, steak, Thai green curry or a selection from the specials board. Telephone: 01784 482000.

THE WALK

After admiring the nearby windmill now available as a holiday let, leave the car park and turn left along **The Green**. At the road junction, turn right along **Windsor Road**, passing **The Grange** on your left and the **George Inn** on your right.

Records of 1731 indicate that the George Inn was a meeting place on 'staking day'. This is thought to refer to a day when strips of land were allocated to the farmers in the area. The records also indicate that a forfeit of one shilling was charged for non-attendance at the meeting.

In 150 yards turn left along **St Andrew's Close**. Go through the lych gate and keep on the path to the left of **St Andrew's Church**, following it round towards the entrance porch on the right.

St Andrew's church dates from the early part of the 13th century. It was extensively restored and refaced in 1862 but the chancel arch is 13th

century, as are sections of the font. The oak pulpit dates from the late 17th century. Amongst those buried in the church is one Edward Gould, a servant of King Charles II.

Just before reaching the entrance porch, turn left through the churchyard to a kissing gate. Go through this and cross the field to reach another kissing gate. With a stream now on your left, continue ahead along an enclosed path. After passing through another kissing gate, the path veers away from the stream to reach yet another gate. As you head across the next field directly ahead, on top of Coopers Hill, you should be able to see the white top of the **Air Forces Memorial**.

The Air Forces Memorial, constructed in 1953, commemorates over 20,000 airmen who were killed during the Second World War and who have no known grave. The designer, Sir Edward Maufe, also designed Guildford cathedral. In the Runnymede meadows below the memorial can be found the Magna Carta Memorial and the John F. Kennedy Memorial. The latter stands in a field given to the USA in 1965.

Drive and Stroll

At the far side of the field, cross over a footbridge, through a gate, and continue ahead along the edge of the next field to reach a drive.

 ③

Turn left here and cross a lane, diagonally left, to a gate leading into the **Ankerwycke Estate**, now owned by the National Trust. Go through the gate and head straight across the middle of the field. At the far side, go through a gate and turn left along the field edge. Go through a gate on the left and ahead to reach a track T-junction. Turn right. As the ruins of **Ankerwycke Priory** come into view, the yew tree is on the left.

It is recorded that, about 1160, Ankerwycke Priory owned an estate in Wraysbury, which was endowed by its founder Gilbert de Mountfichet. During the 13th century Ankerwycke Priory housed a commune of Benedictine nuns. The grounds overlook the River Thames and Magna Carta Island, where King John affixed his seal to the 'Magna Carta' in 1215. The growth of trees and foliage hides the island today. It is reputed that the ancient yew tree, near the nunnery, was the location of a clandestine meeting between Henry VIII and Anne Boleyn.

Carry on past the ruins to reach the trees on the bank of the **River Thames**. Now turn left. The path runs fairly close to the river, which will be on your right. Between the trees you will have good views of the Runnymede meadows over on the opposite side before the river bends to the left.

 ④

On reaching a brick wall, turn left along an enclosed path that emerges at a road at the far end.

 ⑤

Cross the road, **with care**, and turn right, passing the entrance to the British Airways Sailing Club. At **Hythe End**, follow the road round a sharp left-hand bend **(Wraysbury Road)**. Just after going over the **Colne Brook**, look for a footpath sign on the left.

 ⑥

Turn left down a few steps, over a stile, to follow a path that runs between the **Colne Brook**, on your left, and **Wraysbury Lake**, on your right. At the far end continue ahead to reach a stile beside the Windsor to Staines railway line. Note the warning sign – **Stop, Look, Listen** – before crossing.

 ⑦

Cross the stile at the far side and turn left along an enclosed path that runs parallel to the railway. The high banks of **Wraysbury reservoir** can be seen through the railings on your right. When the **Colne Brook** comes

The nunnery ruins at Ankerwycke

back into view, the path veers right to emerge at a road.

Turn left over the railway bridge then turn left down some steps to the **Wraysbury station** approach road. At the bottom turn right to rejoin the main road again. Continue ahead for 100 yards to reach **Tithe Lane** on the left.

Turn left, passing **Tithe Farm**, and at the far end of the lane continue

along an enclosed path that runs at the back of some gardens. A sailing lake can be seen on your left. Bear right at a path junction to emerge at a road. Cross the road to **Wraysbury Baptist church** opposite and turn right. Pass the **Perseverance public house** and immediately turn left into a short side road. Keep to the left to cross over a small wooden footbridge. Pass **Orange Cottage** and the entrance to the Windmill and then turn left into the car park to finish the walk.

Place of Interest Nearby

Runnymede Meadows have been associated with civil liberty ever since King John signed the Magna Carta in 1215. Here you will find the Magna Carta Memorial and the John F. Kennedy Memorial. The latter was erected in 1965. There is also a tearoom nearby.

2 | Eton Wick and Eton

The Walk 5 miles ⏱ 3 hours
Map OS Explorer 160 – Windsor, Weybridge & Bracknell (GR 948784)

How to get there

From Slough, take the A332 south towards Windsor. After passing under the M4, at a roundabout continue straight ahead into Eton. At a set of traffic lights, turn right and follow the B3026 to Eton Wick. The village hall, where the walk starts, is on the left just before a parade of shops.
Parking: This is available in nearby service roads or at the sports club car park near the village hall.

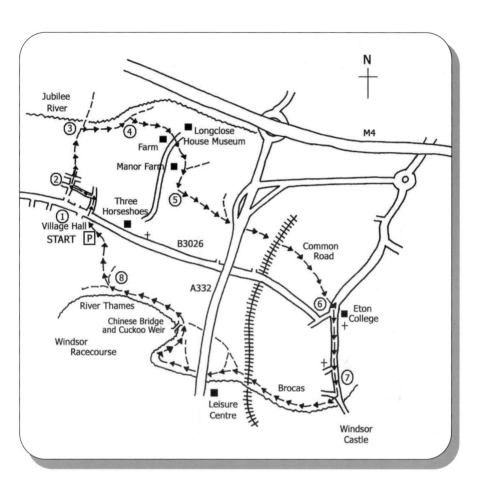

Introduction

This level walk provides the walker with the opportunity of seeing the Jubilee River, Eton College, the Brocas and excellent views of Windsor Castle. Those familiar with stamp collecting will recognise these views as they have been used on high value postage stamps. The return to Eton Wick follows a section of the River Thames towpath. When open, there is also an opportunity to visit the History on Wheels Museum, which is passed on the walk. The museum contains old vehicles, many of which have been used in major film and TV productions.

Drive and Stroll

The Three Horseshoes

The pub is situated on the B3026, not far from the start of the walk in the direction of Eton. The inn serves traditional cask ales including John Smith's. The food menu includes soup, prawn cocktail, fresh meat or fish dishes. Telephone: 01753 867889

THE WALK

With your back to the village hall, cross the B3026 and go along **Bell Lane** opposite. After passing **Bellsfield Court** flats, turn left into **Alma Road**.

At the road junction, at the far end, turn right **(Moores Lane)**. Where this bends left continue straight ahead to pass between two metal posts. Now follow an enclosed path until you reach the **Jubilee River**.

The Jubilee River was created to alleviate flooding in the area, caused by the River Thames overflowing. The channel, excavated between 1996 and 2001, leaves the Thames at Maidenhead and rejoins it again at Datchet.

Do not cross the bridge over the river. Turn right, between barriers. Walk along the wide track, keeping the river on your left, until a wooden fence starts on the left.

Here, turn right over a stile. Cross a small field. Go over a second stile and bear left along the field edge. At a footpath sign, continue straight ahead towards **Eton Common Farm**. Pass to the left of the farm. At a garden corner, bear slightly right to reach a stile and lane. To your left is the entrance to **Longclose House** and the **History on Wheels Museum**.

The History on Wheels Museum is only open on Bank Holidays and on one Sunday a month between March and December. There is also a shop and a NAAFI canteen on site. Telephone: 01753 862637.

Cross the stile on the opposite side of the lane and go through three fields to reach a footpath junction. Turn right along a track. Where this bends right, to **Manor Farm**, continue straight ahead to reach another path/track junction.

Turn left along the field edge. At a T-junction, turn right, then left to pass under the A332. On the other side, the track bends left, then right towards a railway viaduct. Pass under the railway and continue ahead along **Common Road**. At a junction, bear right and follow the road between Eton College buildings to reach the junction with **Slough Road**.

Henry VI founded Eton College in 1440; its Perpendicular Gothic chapel, completed in 1487, contains some fine Flemish-style wall paintings and is well worth a visit.

Turn right along **Slough Road**. The entrance into the main college and to the chapel is on your left. At the traffic lights continue straight ahead along the **High Street** and into the centre of Eton. Note the numbers on the doors. They run consecutively rather than alternatively like most streets. Also note the old stocks and Victorian post box outside the **Tiger Garden**. The building, which dates back to 1420, was previously known as 'the Cockpit'.

Just before reaching the bridge, turn right along **Brocas Street**. Keep to the left of the **Watermans Arms**, then right of Eton College Boathouse, to reach the Brocas. Continue ahead across the Brocas following the Thames Path. The path passes under Telford's railway bridge and then under the Windsor relief road. Beyond the road bridge the river makes a wide right-hand sweep. You can either keep to the towpath, or you can cut the corner, either way both paths meet up at **Chinese Bridge**. This curved wooden bridge takes you over **Cuckoo Weir**. Continue on the Thames Path until you reach another small bridge and footpath sign. Over on the opposite side of the Thames you should be able to see **Windsor Racecourse**.

.

Do not cross the bridge. Turn right here, keeping the **Boveney Ditch** on your left. At a multi-footpath sign, continue straight ahead towards the buildings of **Eton Wick**. Keep to the right-hand edge of a sports field to reach a road **(Haywards Mead)**. Turn left to return to **Eton Wick Village Hall**, which is just past the Sports Club.

Place of Interest Nearby

Windsor Castle is the largest inhabited castle in the world. Its attractions include St George's chapel, Queen Mary's dolls house and the state apartments. Telephone: 0207 766 7304.

3 Swinley Park

The Walk 4¹/₂ miles ⏱ 2¹/₂ hours
Map OS Explorer 160 – Windsor, Weybridge & Bracknell (GR 901683)

How to get there

From Ascot, take the A329 towards Bracknell. At the second set of traffic lights turn left along the B3017. Pass the entrance into Lavender Park Golf Centre and look for an entrance on the left leading to Englemere Pond car park. If you reach the bridge over the railway line you have gone too far. **Parking:** Englemere Pond (free) car park.

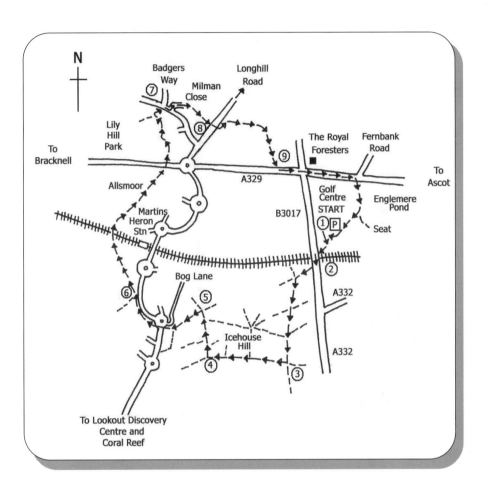

Introduction

This delightful walk takes you through part of Swinley Park, which is owned by the Crown Estate. The Park is a Site of Special Scientific Interest (SSSI) due to its rare insect species and ancient broad-leaved trees. The route then uses a cycle path that takes you through East Bracknell and Martin's Heron before entering the landscaped Lily Hill Park. On the return leg the route passes close to Englemere Pond, another designated SSSI, noted for its rare wetland plants.

Drive and Stroll

The Royal Foresters Hotel

The hotel, situated at the junction of the A329 and B3017, has facilities that include a Beefeater restaurant. Bar meals and a varied restaurant menu are available: the choice is yours. It is a popular venue and it is advisable to book at weekends and bank holidays, if you intend to use the restaurant. Telephone: 01344 884747.

THE WALK

Facing the car park exit, bear left to pick up a path beside a metal gate. In 40 yards, at a cross path, turn right to reach the B3017. Turn left along the road and over the railway. In 150 yards, look for a swing gate leading into **Swinley Park**.

Turn right, through the gate, and walk along a wide track to reach a multi-track junction. Look out for **Ramblers Route** discs on wooden posts. You will be following this route for about 1^1/$_2$ miles. At the junction, turn left and in a further 20 yards turn left again. Go straight over the first two cross tracks, continuing ahead until you reach a third cross track.

Turn right here. In 300 yards, look for a semi-circle of lime trees on the right which marks the entrance to where Swinley Lodge once stood. In a further 100 yards, at the top of a small rise called **Ice House Hill**, there is another circle of limes,

which mark roughly where the Lodge Ice House was sited. Continue ahead along the track.

Where the track starts to bend left, veer right down a grassy track. In 30 yards, turn right. Remain on this track until you reach the next cross track junction.

Turn left here along a wide ride. At the far end, where the ride bends to the left, veer right to go through a swing gate in the boundary fence. Go ahead for 15 yards to reach **Bog Lane**. Turn left to reach the **B3430** at a roundabout. Cross the road to the far side, using the traffic island, and turn right along **New Forest Ride**. Pass a small traffic island and continue for about 80 yards to reach the second of two cycle route signs.

Bear left along a metalled cycle track and remain on it, ignoring all bridges going over a ditch on your left, until you reach a tunnel under the railway. Go through the tunnel and continue along **Allsmoor Lane**

on the far side, passing a pond to your left. On reaching the A329, go directly across, using the zebra crossing, and through the barrier opposite into Lily Hill Park. Follow a gradually ascending path. At the top, bear left, then turn right passing a small wooden bench seat. In a further 80 yards, turn right up some steps and, just after a left-hand bend, turn right and follow a path down to reach a road, with **Badger's Way** just opposite.

 ⑦

Turn right and, in 50 yards, turn left into **Milman Close**. At the far end, continue ahead along a footpath through some trees. Go straight over a cross path and up the bank opposite to reach a field. Keep to the right-hand edge of the field following it round to the right to reach a car park at the far side. There is a mast and small skateboard park to the right.

 ⑧

Leave the car park via its main entrance and turn left along **Long Hill Road**. In 20 yards, turn right across the road to a footpath on the opposite side. Now follow a winding path through the trees. Soon a wire fence appears on your right. The path remains fairly close to the fence, bending right and descending to eventually emerge at the **A329 Ascot-Bracknell** road.

 ⑨

Turn left towards the traffic lights. Go straight across and continue along the A329, passing the **Royal Foresters Hotel** and then the **Licensed Victualler's School**, both on your left.

 ⑩

At the next set of traffic lights (**Fernbank Road** on left), turn right across the zebra crossing. Bear left to reach and go through a gate on the right. Follow a path through the trees, ignoring a path going left, until you reach a path junction. Directly ahead is **Englemere Pond**. Bear right to reach a wider and clearer path. Bear right along this path (**Ramblers Route**). Continue along the Ramblers Route path for a short distance, with the boundary of the **Lavender Park Golf Centre** over to your right, before veering right, over duckboards, to return to the car park.

Places of Interest Nearby

The Look Out Discovery Centre, situated just off the B3430 south-west of this walk, includes an adventure playground, a picnic area, and over 2,000 acres of woodland. There is also a coffee and gift shop and the centre is open daily between 10 am and 5 pm. Telephone: 01344 354400.

4 Cookham Dean Common

Cookham Dean Common

The Walk 3 miles 🕒 2 hours
Map OS Explorer 160 – Windsor, Weybridge & Bracknell (GR 862843)

How to get there

From Maidenhead, take the A308 towards Marlow. At Pinkneys Green, veer right onto a minor road (Winter Hill Road), signed to Cookham Dean. Pass Choke Lane, on the right, and in 300 yards look for a small lay-by on the right, at the edge of the Common. **Parking:** In the lay-by (owned by the National Trust).

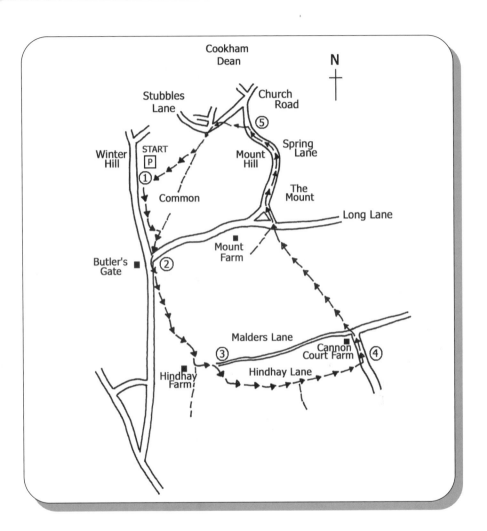

Introduction

Cookham Dean Common, together with a number of other Cookham and Maidenhead commons totalling some 850 acres, was acquired by public funding and handed over to the National Trust in 1934. This circular walk takes in part of the Common, goes through woodland and crosses farmland, from where there is a good view looking towards Cliveden, on the Buckingham side of the River Thames. There is one gradual, but gentle, ascent.

Drive and Stroll

Uncle Tom's Cabin

Although there is no pub on the route of the walk, this cosy cottage-style inn is situated in Hills Lane, Cookham Dean, about a mile from the start of the walk. Renovated during the 1980s, it has managed to retain its 17th-century character and charm. There is a large garden at the rear. A varied menu includes Cajun chicken, steak and ale pie and seafood dishes. Lunch is not served on Mondays. Telephone: 01628 483339.

THE WALK

###

With your back to the road, step onto the common and immediately turn right, walking parallel to the road. After passing a large tree on the common, the path veers left to reach the edge of a strip of woodland. Turn right through the trees, ignoring a path going left, to reach **Choke Lane**. Cross the road and turn right. At the road junction, turn left along **Winter Lane Road** for 40 yards to reach a footpath on the left.

###

Bear left through the trees. At a junction, fork left and ignoring a path on the left follow a meandering path through the woods until you reach a path junction and the wooden fence of a compound. Turn left to pass between a barrier and the corner of the compound and continue ahead, with a wire fence on your right, to reach an open field. Turn right along the field edge towards **Hindhay Farm**. At the field corner, go ahead through a gap to reach a track **(Malders Lane)**.

###

Turn left along this gravel track. Ahead you can see the mound of a fairly large reservoir. In 100 yards, where a footpath crosses the track, turn right. Go through a swing gate and bear left across a field. Go through the swing gate on the opposite side and turn left down **Hindhay Lane**. Ignoring paths going off right, follow the lane down until you reach a minor road **(Cannon Court Road)**.

###

Turn left along the road, passing **Cannon Court Farm** on your left. Where the road bends right, ignore **Malders Lane** on the left and continue straight ahead up a track, running between wire fences. Looking to your right there is a good view across the Thames Valley to the woodland of the **Cliveden Estate**, on the Buckinghamshire side of the River Thames. Amongst the trees you should be able to see the mansion house.

Court Farm

The Cliveden estate, overlooking the River Thames, has a series of gardens, each having its own character. The Italianate mansion house is the third to be built on the site. Charles Barry built the present house for the Duke of Sutherland in 1851. It was once the home of Lady Astor. Today, the house serves as a hotel.

Where the fence on the left ends continue straight ahead. As the track gradually ascends you can see, again to your right, the houses of Cookham Rise and, just beyond, those of Cookham. Go through a gap and continue up through a field. Pass through a open gate to reach a road. Cross this and continue up **Spring Lane** opposite, passing the entrance to **The Mount**, on the right. At a junction, continue straight ahead. Take care along this stretch, as there are no verges to walk along. At the top continue along the road until you reach a sharp bend, with **Pudseys Close**, on the left.

Turn left here. Follow the drive between houses to its end. Now continue straight ahead, passing through a wooden barrier, to follow an enclosed path down to reach another drive. There is a house named **Darbys** on your left. Turn right to emerge at a road (Church Road). Turn left down the road, ignoring a path going across the green on your right. Continue ahead, passing **Stubbles Lane** on the right. The road now becomes a track. Where this bends right, at a footpath junction, continue straight ahead through the trees to emerge at the edge of **Cookham Dean Common**. Bear right across the common to return to the car park.

Places of Interest Nearby

Cookham has a long association with the artist Stanley Spencer. In 1962 a former Methodist chapel on the corner of the High Street and the A4094 was converted and became the **Stanley Spencer Gallery**. In addition to displaying exhibits of his paintings the gallery contains a permanent collection of his notes, letters and documents. Telephone: 01628 471885.

5 White Waltham

The Walk $5^3/_4$ miles ⏱ $2^1/_2$ hours
Map OS Explorer 160 – Windsor, Weybridge & Bracknell (GR 849772)

How to get there

Leave the A404(M) at junction 9a, signed to Cox Green. Drive through Cox Green and on to Woodlands Park. At a staggered T-junction, turn left into Waltham Road and follow it through the village. As you round a sharp left-hand turn, you will see a sports field on the right. The Beehive public house is on the left. **Parking:** The inn car park for patrons but please seek the landlord's permission before leaving your car whilst you walk.

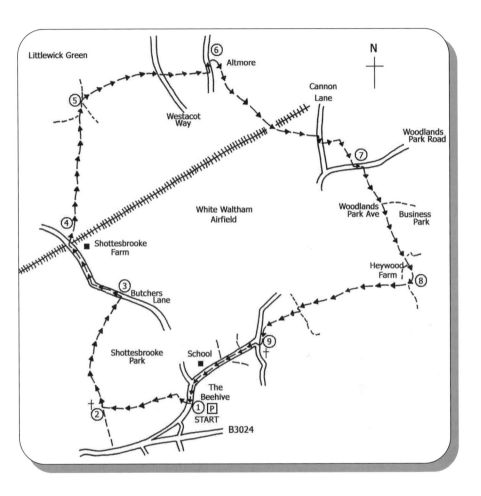

Introduction

The settlement of White Waltham dates back to at least the Saxon era; possibly even to Roman times. The village, together with Shottesbrooke and Waltham St Lawrence, existed as one estate under the title of Waltham. The fact that Waltham Abbey, Essex, once owned the village is considered to be coincidental. After leaving the village, this level walk visits Shottesbrooke Park before heading north towards Littlewick Green. The return to White Waltham crosses over the main London-Reading railway line where you can watch the trains and/or the planes that land at nearby White Waltham airfield.

Drive and Stroll

The Beehive

The inn is an ideal venue, especially in the summer, when you can sit, supping your ale and watching a cricket match on the sports field opposite. The interior is decorated with wallpaper that has bees included in its pattern. A plaque on the wall outside reports that the inn burnt down in May 1861; it was rebuilt in June 1861. Bar snacks are available in addition to more substantial meals. Beers include Brakspear, Abbot, and a guest ale. Telephone: 01628 822877.

THE WALK

Leave the inn car park and turn left. In 50 yards, just past **Walgrove Gardens**, turn right across the road. Go through a gap in the hedge and bear right behind the sports club. Follow the left-hand edge of the sports field to reach a footpath sign. Turn left, here and follow a path leading to a stile at the edge of Shottesbrooke Park. Go over the stile and cross the park towards **Shottesbrooke church**.

Built by Sir William Trussell during the 14th century, St John the Baptist's church takes its design from that of Salisbury cathedral. The founder and his wife are buried in the north transept. Inside you will find that the chancel is actually longer than the nave.

On reaching a drive, turn right. Pass **Shottesbrooke Park House** on the left and, where the drive bends left,

continue straight ahead across the parkland. On reaching an old grassy drive bear right and follow it through an avenue of trees to reach **Butchers Lane**.

Turn left along the lane. Pass **Shottesbrooke Farm** on your right and continue ahead, over the railway bridge.

On the other side, turn right at a footpath sign and, in 20 yards, turn left across a large field, heading towards a distant hedgerow. At the far side, turn right along a metalled track, following it around a left-hand bend and ignoring a path going off to the right.

At the next corner, with a gate ahead, turn right. (However, if you want to visit **Littlewick Green**, one-time home of the composer Ivor Novello, continue ahead, through the gate and follow the path to the village. This will add about $1/2$ mile to the walk.) The metalled track now follows a line of telegraph posts to reach a road **(Westacott Way)**. Go straight across and continue along the track the other side to reach another road, with a house called **Altmore** just opposite. Turn left here.

 ⑥

In 120 yards, turn sharp right into **Breadcroft Lane**. Pass Barn House and the Cherry Garden Nursing Home, both on the right, and continue along the lane until you reach the bridge over the railway. Continue along the minor road to reach **Cannon Lane**. Turn right and, in 60 yards, turn left into **Smithfield Road**, following it round to reach a T-junction.

 ⑦

Turn left along **Woodlands Park Road**. In 100 yards turn right along **Woodlands Park Avenue**. Pass the buildings of Woodland Park Business Park, on your left, and continue along a track **(Snowball Hill)**. Ignore a footpath going left and go ahead to reach **Heywood Farm**.

 ⑧

Just beyond the farm the track bends to the right. Ignore a track going left and continue ahead between narrow metal posts to follow a wide track. Where this bends right, turn left along a concrete track. There is a small works enclosure on your left. In 25 yards turn right through a gap to follow a path between fields. At a hedge corner continue straight ahead. **White Waltham church** can be seen over to your left.

 ⑨

Cross a stile at the far side and immediately turn left along a path running parallel with the road. It emerges at a road junction.

(If you wish to visit White Waltham church, turn left up the hill. Buried in the churchyard is Sir Constantine Phipps who became Lord Chancellor of Ireland. He died in 1723.)

Turn right, across the road to the pavement on the opposite side, then turn left and follow the road, through the village, back to the Beehive public house, which will be on your left.

Place of Interest Nearby

Braywick Park and Nature Centre, Maidenhead – The park contains a number of old trees, which can be seen from the pathways including a Tree Trail and a Nature Trail. To get there from White Waltham, reverse your journey back to Cox Green and continue over the A404(M) into Maidenhead. Turn right along the A308 towards Windsor and look for Braywick Park (Hibbert Road) on the left. Telephone 01628 777440 or 01628 796227 for details.

6 Gardeners Green

The Walk 4 miles 2¹/₂ hours
Map OS Explorer 159 – Reading, Wokingham & Pangbourne (GR 798762)

How to get there

From the A329 ring road (Peach Street) in Wokingham, head south-east along Easthampstead Road. After passing under the railway and a drive on the right leading to Ludgrove School, turn right along Heathlands Road. Pass a Craft Village and turn left along Honey Hill to reach the Crooked Billet public house. **Parking:** Patrons may park in the pub car park, but please obtain the landlord's permission before leaving your car there while you walk. Alternative parking can be found at the Holme Grange Craft Village (near point 2 of the walk) which is open from 10 am to 5 pm all year except from 25th December to 1st January inclusive.

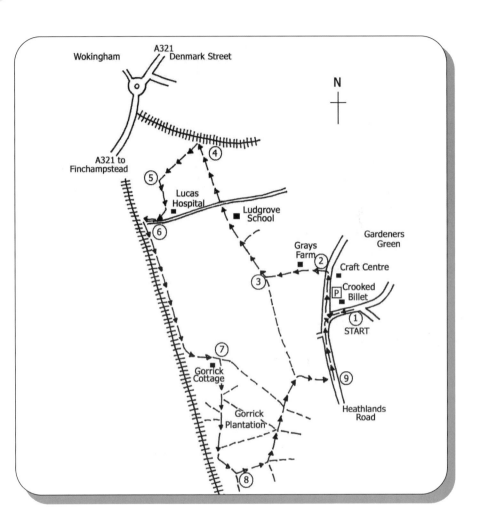

Introduction

Gardeners Green, with its farms, nurseries, garden centre and craft village, all but lives up to its name, so, if your partner does not want to accompany you on this walk, there is plenty to keep them occupied. Heading towards Wokingham, this level walk takes you past Ludgrove School, where the royal princes, William and Harry, are listed amongst its past pupils. The route then turns south and finally goes through the woodland of Gorrick Plantation before returning to the Crooked Billet public house.

Drive and Stroll

The Crooked Billet

This is a popular country pub, with a weatherboard façade. Internal modifications have taken place fairly recently and its décor and furnishings give it a warm and cosy feeling. The comprehensive menu includes sandwiches, baguettes, bangers and mash, and liver and bacon amongst the choices on offer. Booking is advisable for the evenings and for Sunday lunch. No food is available on Sunday evenings. The pub has a garden and a small play area. Telephone: 01189 780438.

THE WALK

Leave the inn car park and turn right along **Honey Hill**. At the road junction, turn right into **Heathlands Road**. Pass the entrance to **Holme Grange Craft Village**, on the right, and continue along the road for another 80 yards to reach the entrance to **Grays Farm** on the opposite side of the road.

Over 150 local craft-workers and artists exhibit their work in a Craft Barn and Art Gallery within the Holme Grange Craft Village. The Craft Barn is a converted 19th-century milking barn, which has its original wooden beams and cast iron milking bays still intact. The Village also has a herb garden, and a 'Tea Shoppe' selling home made cream teas and snacks.

Cross the road, **with care**, and follow the track towards the farm. Pass to the left of the farm buildings (you

may even see a 6ft strawberry nearby) and keep to the track as it bends left, then right before passing between farm produce to reach a gate in the far left corner of the field.

Turn right here and follow a path running between trees and bushes. On reaching the entrance to Ludgrove School playing field on the left, the path becomes a track. In 30 yards, where the track bends right into the grounds of **Ludgrove School**, veer left at a footpath sign. The school is well hidden by trees and you will not get a good view of it.

Ludgrove School, which moved to its current site in 1937, is one of the best-known preparatory schools in the country. Its fame was enhanced during the period when Prince William and Prince Harry were pupils there. Amongst its array of former pupils are the Duke of Devonshire and Sir Alec Douglas Home.

Follow an enclosed path through the trees, keeping the school boundary on your right, until you reach a drive. Go straight across and continue along the path on the other side. The path, much wider now, crosses over a stream and passes under telegraph wires, before it reaches a footbridge over a railway line.

Just before reaching the railway bridge, turn sharp left (FPS) over a stile. Follow a narrow path, with a wire fence on your left and a small ditch on your right. It can get very muddy and wet here following heavy rain. *(If the path is waterlogged retrace your steps to the drive near Ludgrove School and turn right along the drive to reach the Lucas hospital building (see point 5) where you can rejoin the walk).* If the path is clear you will reach a footbridge over a small stream. Cross this and continue across a paddock. Go through a barrier and along the left-hand edge of the next field to reach a track.

Turn left along the track. Pass to the right of **Chapel Green Farm** and continue straight ahead along a metalled road. Where this bends right, with the old **Lucas Hospital** on your left, go straight ahead to a stile. Cross this and look back to your left to get a good view of this impressive and attractive building.

During the 17th century, Henry Lucas, a mathematician and Member of Parliament for Cambridge University, left £7,000 for the foundation of a hospital that would provide shelter for a number of poor men in Berkshire. The result was the erection, in 1666, of this building that became known as the Lucas Hospital. The hospital still cares for the elderly today but it is run more as a retirement home.

Bear right across a small field to reach the Ludgrove School drive. Turn right, passing through the drive entrance, to reach a wide track on the left.

Turn left along this byway for just over $1/2$ mile. The track runs parallel to a railway line over to your right. Keep to the main track when it bends left, passing a barn on the left and, just beyond, **Gorrick Cottage**. Continue ahead between fences for 80 yards to reach a track on the right.

Turn right between some small posts and follow the track through the trees. At a track/path junction continue straight ahead along a wide track. Ignore tracks going off left and right until you reach a sharp left-hand bend. Remain on the main track, around the bend, to reach a track junction.

Drive and Stroll

 ⑧

Fork left here and, ignoring a path going off left, continue to the next junction. Keep to the main track as it bends left and gradually ascend a small rise. Ignore a path on the left, go straight over a cross track and continue ahead to reach a barrier and cross track. Go straight across and continue ahead on a narrow path. Just after crossing over a wooden footbridge you reach a footpath junction. Turn right here and follow another narrow path until you emerge at a road.

 ⑨

Turn left along the road. Pass **Holly Cottage Nursery**, on the left, and **Wyevale Garden Centre**, on the right, to reach a road on the right. Turn right into **Honey Hill** and follow the road back to the Crocked Billet public house, which will be on your left.

Place of Interest Nearby

Dinton Pastures Country Park, situated about 4 miles north-west of Wokingham. The lakes were created when old gravel pits were flooded to create an attractive recreational area. The 350-acre park, officially opened in 1979, attracts many visitors who come to enjoy bird watching, fishing, water sports, nature trails and orienteering. There are picnic areas within the grounds and also a café where refreshments can be purchased. Telephone: 0118 934 2016.

7 | Ruscombe and Twyford

The River Loddon

The Walk 4$\frac{1}{2}$ miles ⏱ 2$\frac{1}{2}$ hours
Map OS Explorer 159 – Reading, Wokingham & Pangbourne (GR 798762)

How to get there

From the A4 at Hare Hatch, take the A3032 towards Twyford branching off left to get to Ruscombe. At a crossroads in Ruscombe, turn left along the B3024 and where this bends left go directly ahead to reach Ruscombe church. **Parking:** There is limited parking near the church.

Drive and Stroll

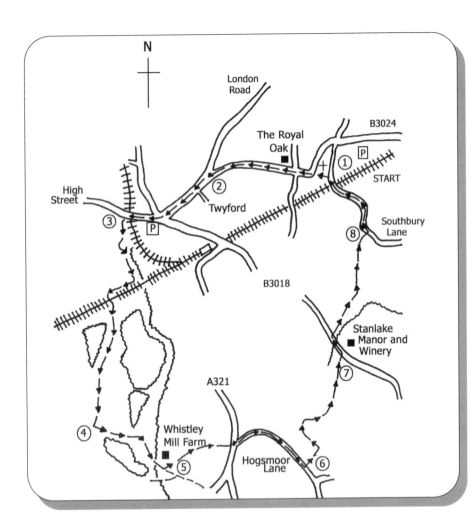

Introduction

This delightful walk starts from the village of Ruscombe where William Penn, the founder of Pennsylvania, lived from 1710 until his death in 1718. It is thought that his route to his Quaker meetings in Reading took him through Twyford, and this walk may even follow the route he took into Twyford. Heading south between the Twyford lakes, the route then turns east to visit Stanlake, where there is an opportunity to sample local wines at Stanlake Wine Estate.

The Royal Oak

This local inn caters for diners by providing light snacks through to full dinners. Beers include London Pride and Young's Bitter. Food is available daily between 12 noon and 2.30 pm and from 7 pm to 9.30 pm (Sunday between 12 noon and 4 pm). Telephone: 01189 780438.

THE WALK

Facing **Ruscombe church** (south side) turn left along the lane. At the main road junction (B3024) continue straight ahead and again at the crossroads. Pass the **Royal Oak public house**, on your right, and continue down **Ruscombe Road** to reach a road junction.

Bear left along **London Road** into Twyford. Just before reaching the traffic lights you will pass the Thai Elephant restaurant, which may have two small elephants standing outside. At the lights go straight ahead, along the **High Street**. Pass the **Duke of Wellington pub** and **Polehampton Close**, both on your left. Continue ahead over the Twyford to Henley railway line to reach **Silk Lane** (FPS).

In Polehampton Close there is a car park (free on Sundays) and toilets. The name Polehampton is attributed to an Edward Polehampton who, in 1666, as a destitute boy was taken in by a local innkeeper. He prospered and grew rich. When he died he bequeathed a charity to benefit the poor boys of the village. The Wee Waif inn on the A4 is named in memory of him.

Turn left along a path, over **Weavers Way**, and down some steps opposite. Go over a footbridge and turn left to pass between a small stream and some flats. Pass a noticeboard and continue ahead to reach a small weir. Cross the bridge over the weir and turn left to follow a path that runs alongside the **River Loddon**, on your left. Just before reaching a railway viaduct, the path veers right then left to reach a footpath junction. Turn left through a tunnel under the railway and continue ahead at the far side. Pass a small car park, on the left, and carry straight on to reach a road.

Turn left here and, in 40 yards, join a footpath on the right that runs parallel to the road. Where the path joins the road, cross over, and carry on along the footpath that continues on the other side. On rejoining the road go straight on to reach **Whistley Bridge**.

Drive and Stroll

Ignoring a footpath on the right continue along the road for 80 yards.

At a bridleway sign, turn left along a fenced track. At the far end, cross over the **A321** and continue along **Hogmore Lane** opposite. Follow the lane as it bends right. Shortly after passing a small footbridge on the right look for a footpath sign on the left.

Turn left, through a gap, and head across a field towards some woodland. Go over a small footbridge on the far side and fork left along a path that runs just inside the wood edge, with a ditch to your left. The path swings right to reach another footbridge. Cross this, then a stile, and immediately turn right along the field edge, with the wood now on your right. Go through a gap (it can get muddy here) and continue along the edge of the next field to reach a road **(B3018)**. The entrance to **Stanlake Wine Estate** is 50 yards on your right.

The origins of the Stanlake Estate date back to the 12th century, when the Earl of Salisbury held the land. The estate was then known then as Hinton Pipard. During the 15th century the estate passed to the Thorpe family. When their daughter Elizabeth married Nicholas Stanlake, the estate, name changed from Hinton Pipard to Stanlake Park. In the late 1970s Jon Leighton decided to create a 25-acre vineyard, known then as Thames Valley Vineyard.

Turn left along the road and over the bridge. In a further 70 yards, at a footpath sign, turn right over a stile. Cross the field, keeping to the left of some mid-field trees. Go over a farm track and across the next field, with a fence on your left. There is a good view of **Stanlake Manor** over to your right. At the far side, go over a stile and footbridge and head across the next field, towards a red-bricked house, to reach a road.

Turn left along this minor road, over the railway and back to Ruscombe church.

Place of Interest Nearby

The **Berkshire Museum of Aviation,** Mohawk Way, Woodley, has a fascinating collection of aircraft and photographs recalling Berkshire's aviation history. The museum is open all year but times vary. Telephone: 0118 944 8089.

8 | California Country Park

California's 6-acre lake

The Walk 3¹/₄ miles 🕐 2 hours
Map OS Explorer 159 – Reading, Wokingham & Pangbourne (GR 784650)

How to get there

From Wokingham, take the A321 south through Eastheath. At a roundabout, take the B3016, signed to Finchhampstead. At a staggered junction with the B3430, turn right for just over ¹/₂ mile to reach the entrance to California Country Park, on the right. Follow the drive to reach a car park on the left. **Parking:** The car park is usually free on weekdays but there is a small charge at weekends and bank holidays.

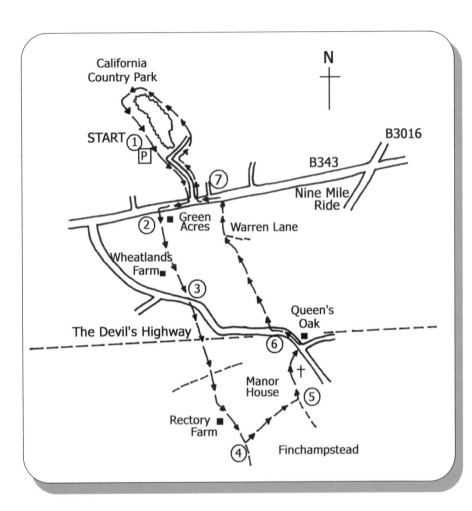

Introduction

This fairly level walk takes you south of the park, where you have an opportunity to see, or visit, Finchampstead church. You can also visit the Queen's Oak inn, which is close to the church. Returning to the park the route takes you round Longmoor Lake before returning to the car park. There is a café and some picnic areas near the lake.

The Queen's Oak

The inn obtained its current name from an oak tree that was planted on the green in 1897 in honour of Queen Victoria's diamond jubilee. With the Devils Highway, the old Roman Road that ran from Silchester to London, passing nearby it is thought that there may have been a hostelry here in Roman times. The present building is partly Tudor. The 16th-century main door was once the porch door of St James's church. The pub's earlier name, the White Horse, is a reminder of the times when it was a coaching inn. Brakspear ales are on offer, and food ranges from steak and ale pie to Cajun chicken, gammon or steaks. Children under 14 are welcome to use the garden but not the bars. Telephone: 0118 973 4855.

THE WALK

(1)

Leave the car park and walk down the drive back to the main entrance. Turn right along the pavement for about 250 yards to reach the entrance to **Green Acres** on the opposite side.

(2)

Turn left, across the road, to a footpath sign. Keeping to the right-hand side of the entrance, pass a small brick wall on the right to reach a path running between wooden fences. At a timber building, turn left across a concrete drive then turn right past the building to reach a swing gate. Go through this and along the edge of a field, passing a small paddock, and **Wheatlands Farm**, both on the right. Go through another swing gate and across a lane.

(3)

Keep to the left of **Beech Cottage** and continue along the path. Over to your right you may catch a glimpse of **Larchwood Farm**. After going through another gate the path runs along the left-hand edge of three fields. Halfway along the third field a convenient bench seat has been placed so that you can rest and admire the view.

A plaque on the seat reads: 'Summer sun and Winter rain, our lives change just the same. Rest awhile and enjoy the view. We hope the sun will shine on you. – Sandy & Mary Marshall'.

At the far side of the third field, go through a gate to reach a staggered cross path. Continue straight ahead, between wire fences, until you reach the entrance to **Rectory Farm**. Here, the path turns left, then right, as it skirts the farm buildings.

Drive and Stroll

 ④

At the far end of the buildings, turn left along a fenced path. At the far end, go through a gate and over a footbridge. Follow the path as it bends left, then right. Over to your right you should see some of the houses of **Finchampstead** village. At the far end, go up three steps to reach a cross path.

 ⑤

Turn left, up a tree-lined path, to reach a gate. Go through this and up some steps into the churchyard of **St James'** church. Keeping to the left of the church, follow the path round to reach the main entrance.

Finchampstead church is built on the site of an ancient earthwork. The main structure of the church is Norman in origin but its brick tower was added during the 18th century. One of its early doors is reputed to have been taken and installed as one of the front doors of the nearby Queen's Oak pub.

Leave the churchyard through a gap beside a wooden fence and turn right down the road towards a triangular green. Bear left of the green to reach a road junction. The **Queen's Oak** pub is now visible to your left.

It was on this green that, in June 1877, an oak tree was planted to commemorate Queen Victoria's golden jubilee. Thus it was that the nearby inn obtained its current name. The original oak tree did not survive recent storms and you will notice, as you pass, that a new tree has been planted.

Turn left along **White Horse Lane**, passing to the left of the **Queen's Oak**. Go round a left-hand bend and, in 100 yards, look for a footpath on your right.

 ⑥

Turn right, through a gate, and follow an enclosed path between fields, to reach a drive. Turn left and, almost immediately, turn right to reach a road. Cross, with care, and turn left, along the pavement, to reach the entrance to **California Country Park**.

 ⑦

Just before the drive, turn right across the grass, past a telephone kiosk, to join a path that runs parallel to the drive. Keep to the path as it bends right away from the drive and then turn right over a bridge. At the far side, turn right up a concrete path, which soon bends left. Remain on this path until you reach a gate. Do not go through. Turn left following the path round **Longmoor Lake**, which soon becomes visible on your left. On the far side of the lake, pass a small café and information centre, on your right, to return to the car park.

Place of Interest Nearby

California Country Park, owned and run by Wokingham District Council, has 65 acres of woodland in addition to its six-acre lake. The name California derives from California Lodge, a hunting lodge that existed during the period when the area was part of Great Windsor Forest. Nature trails allow you to discover the various species of trees, plants and birds to be found in the park. There are picnic areas and a café within the grounds. Telephone: 0118 934 2016.

9 Shinfield

The Walk 4 miles ⏲ 2 hours
Map OS Explorer 159 – Reading, Wokingham & Pangbourne (GR 733677)

How to get there

Leave the M4 at junction 11 and take the A33 south. At the first roundabout, bear left to go through Three Mile Cross to Spencers Wood. Here, turn left along the B3349 to Shinfield. **Parking:** As you enter the village, the village green and car park will be on your left.

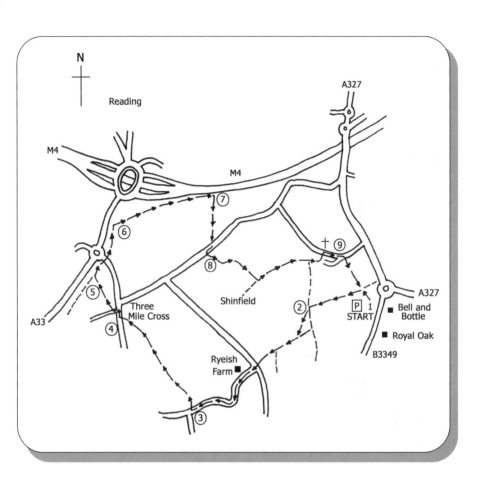

Introduction

Situated 3 miles south of Reading, the settlement of Shinfield dates back to the Saxon era. The village is mentioned in the Domesday Book and its church, St Mary's, was founded in about 1070. The author Mary Mitford describes life in Shinfield in her book *Our Village*. The walk takes you across fields, through the village of Spencers Wood, to the A33, where the route turns north along a pleasant track that runs parallel with the road to its junction with the M4. The route passes close to St Mary's church on the return to Shinfield.

Drive and Stroll

The Bell and Bottle / The Royal Oak

Both these inns, practically next door to each other, are on the opposite side of the road to the village green. Bar food at the Royal Oak is one of its attractions and the menu is varied and comprehensive. It also has a beer garden and play area for children. The Bell and Bottle does not serve food on Mondays. Telephone: The Bell and Bottle 0118 988 3563; the Royal Oak 0118 988 2931.

THE WALK

1. With your back to the main road (B3349), head towards **Shinfield parish hall**. Turn right past the **British Legion** into a field. Now fork left, keeping the building on your left, and head across the field. At the far corner, go up a small bank and, where a path joins from the right, bear left along an enclosed path, with a hedge on your right.

At the far end, bear diagonally left across a concrete farm track to a path that runs between two fields. Follow the path round as it bends right and, ignoring a path on the left, continue towards the houses at **Ryeish Green** where you emerge at a road. Cross the road and continue ahead along **Ryeish Lane** opposite. Some 20 yards before reaching a road junction look for a footpath sign on the right.

Turn right here between metal barriers. Follow the track until you

reach the entrance gate leading into Ryeish Green school sports field. Just before the gate, fork left along a path that passes to the left of a sports pavilion. Continue ahead ignoring all paths going off to the left and continue ahead, keeping the sports field on your right. Go along the right-hand edge of two fields. In the second field, go over a stile on the right and immediately turn left, with a hedge now on your left. Cross a stile in the far corner, and continue along a path that emerges at **Basingstoke Road**.

Cross the road, with care, and turn right. In 50 yards, turn left along **Grazeley Road**. In another 50 yards, at a footpath sign, turn right between houses. Go through a gate and continue ahead along a hedged path. At the far end you reach a track T-junction, with the A33 just beyond.

Turn right along a track that runs parallel with the A33. On reaching a road, with a roundabout to your left, go straight across and continue along a path on the opposite side. This leads to another road, with **Milestone Cottage** just opposite. Note the old white milestone on the pavement in front of the cottage. Turn left towards the A33 and, keeping to the right, pass between small stone pillars to reach a footpath on the right.

Turn right, down and over a footbridge and through a gate into a field. Walk ahead along the right-hand edge of the field which, with the M4 to your left, gradually narrows. The grey 'fortress' of Shire Hall, completed in 1980 can be seen on the far side of the M4. Go through a gap and along the edge of the next field to reach a stile in the far left-hand corner.

Go over the stile and turn right along a fenced path. Go over a small foot-bridge and along the edge of two fields to reach a road. Turn right for 40 yards to reach a footpath on the left.

Turn left alongside a house and garden, then along the edge of a field. Go through a gap and turn left.

At a footpath sign, beside a telegraph post, the path bends right and ascends gradually between fields, keeping to the right of a hedge about halfway up. At the top, at a cross track, turn left towards a new housing estate. Pass between houses and across the first road to continue along **Scobell Road**. Where this bends right, turn left to reach the main road, with **St Mary's church** over to your left.

William Fitzosbern, who was Earl of Hereford at the time, founded St Mary's church about 1070. During a subsidence in the 1930s, a floor brass was revealed. The brass commemorates the parents of Mary Mitford, who lived in Three Mile Cross between 1820 and 1850.

Turn right along **Church Lane**. At the road junction, cross diagonally left to an enclosed path, just to the left of a house called **Stantons**. Pass new houses on the left and straight across a field to return to the British Legion and car park, which you will see ahead of you.

Place of Interest Nearby

Wellington Country Park, situated on the Berkshire/Hampshire border and just to the south of Shinfield, provides a wealth of activities for you to enjoy for the rest of the day. Set in 350 acres of woodland within the Duke of Wellington's estate there are lakes, nature trails, fishing facilities and a gift and coffee shop. Telephone: 0118 932 6444.

10 Sheffield Lock

The Walk $5^{1}/_{2}$ miles 🕒 3 hours
Map OS Explorer 159 – Reading, Wokingham & Pangbourne (GR 648704)

How to get there

Leave the M4 at junction 12 and take the Theale bypass (A4) towards Newbury. Turn left off the bypass following the signs to Theale station, keeping the railway on your left. At the junction, cross over the railway and follow the road to the Kennet and Avon Canal. Just after going over the canal turn left through an entrance leading to a picnic site and car park. **Parking:** Sheffield Lock car park (free).

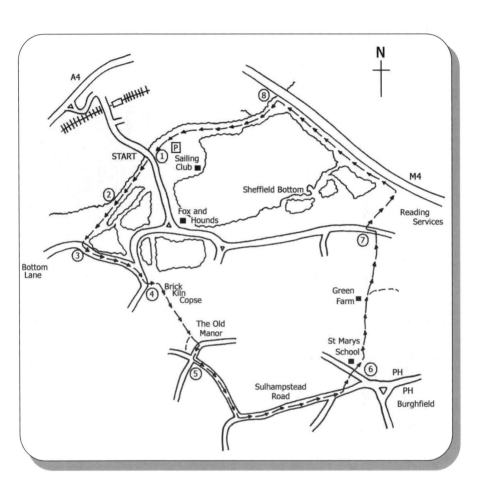

Introduction

The Kennet Canal, between Reading and Newbury, has been open since 1723. Almost a century later, in 1810, it linked up with the Avon Canal, to form the waterway that now runs between Reading and Bath. The canal is rich in wildlife, both flora and fauna. This pleasant walk takes in part of the canal before heading to the village of Burghfield, via field paths and lanes. The return leg skirts Theale Sailing Lake before another stretch of the canal brings you back to the finish.

Drive and Stroll

The Fox and Hounds

The inn was originally built during the mid 19th century and has been recently refurbished and modernised. The dining area is open-plan and caters for families. Being fairly close to the canal and lakes, it attracts many ornithologists, walkers and canal enthusiasts. Beers include Wadworth 6X and 'Summersault', and there is a varied menu. Food is not available on Sunday evenings. Telephone: 0118 930 2295.

THE WALK

Leave the car park via its north-west corner and head towards the **Kennet and Avon Canal**. Turn left along the towpath, passing a sign informing you that it is 13$\frac{1}{2}$ miles to Newbury. Don't worry, you will not be walking that far! Go straight over the road at the swing-bridge, and continue along the towpath on the other side for about $\frac{1}{4}$ mile.

Just before a footbridge over a stream, bear left along a narrow path, leaving the canal towpath. Ignore a gate on the left and continue ahead. Soon you will see a lake on your left and, shortly, a stream and lake on your right. Remain on this path until you reach a road **(Bottom Lane)**.

Turn left along the road until you reach a road junction. Bear right here, following the road until you reach a right-hand bend.

Turn left through a gateway and along a drive leading to a **Highways Training Centre**. Where the drive turns left into the centre, continue ahead past an old wooden garage and fork right up a green track. On reaching an open field, bear slightly left keeping about 30 yards to the right of a pylon. When a house on the far side comes into view, aim just to the right of it to reach a stile. Cross into a small grassy area and go directly ahead, ignoring a gate and stile over to the right. At the far side, just before a gate, turn left. In 5 yards, turn right on an enclosed path which joins the drive leading to the **Old Manor**, which can be seen to your left. Pass between the entrance pillars to reach a minor road. Now bear right to a crossroad.

Turn left in the direction of **Burghfield**. At the next T-junction, turn left again. Pass over Clayhill Brook and continue walking towards the village. Soon you will pass the Stable Door Saddlery, on the right.

At the next road junction, carry straight ahead along Sulhamstead Road, using the pavement on the left. In 100 yards, look for a footpath on the left.

If you wish to visit either the Hatch Gate pub or the Six Bells pub in Burghfield, continue ahead along Sulhamstead Road. To rejoin the walk, return to the road junction and bear right to reach St Mary's school, where you should turn right. See paragraph 6.

The enclosed path runs between gardens to reach a barrier. Go through this and along the edge of a field to reach a road, with **St Mary's C of E primary school** and **School Lane** directly opposite.

Walk along **School Lane**. Where the tarmac surface ends, go over a stile on the left. Now, bear diagonally right across two fields to reach a track near **Green Farm**. Turn right along the

track and, where this bends right, continue ahead along the edge of a couple of fields to reach a road. At the road, turn left.

In 30 yards, turn right along a path that brings you almost to the edge of the M4 motorway. Gravel pits can be seen on your left. At the far end of the path, turn left and follow the enclosed path that runs parallel with the motorway. The path joins a wide track used by lorries carrying gravel from the pits. Continue straight ahead, now with Theale yachting lake visible on your left. Where the track turns left, go straight ahead to reach the **Kennet and Avon Canal**.

At this point, turn left. The route now follows the towpath, passing Garston Lock, back to Sheffield Lock. Before reaching the lock and swing-bridge, veer left to return to the car park and the finish of the walk.

Place of Interest Nearby

The **Museum of English Rural Life**, Redlands Road, Reading, is situated not far from junction 11 of the M4 motorway. The museum has hands-on and interactive displays providing an opportunity to learn about farming, crafts and village life over the last 150 years. It is open Tuesday to Friday, from 10 am to 4.30 pm, but closed on Mondays and open only for a couple of hours on Saturday and Sunday afternoons. Telephone: 0118 378 8660.

11 Padworth Common

Ufton Nervet church

The Walk 4½ miles ⏱ 2½ hours
Map OS Explorer 159 – Reading, Wokingham & Pangbourne (GR 629651)

How to get there

From the A4, just before the A340 Aldermaston roundabout, turn left along Padworth Lane. At a crossroads, go straight ahead (Rectory Road) to reach a triangular junction. Fork left here to join Padworth Road. The Round Oak public house, which has a fairly large car park, is about ½ mile on the right. **Parking:** The inn car park but please check with the landlord before leaving your car whilst you walk. Limited parking is available nearby.

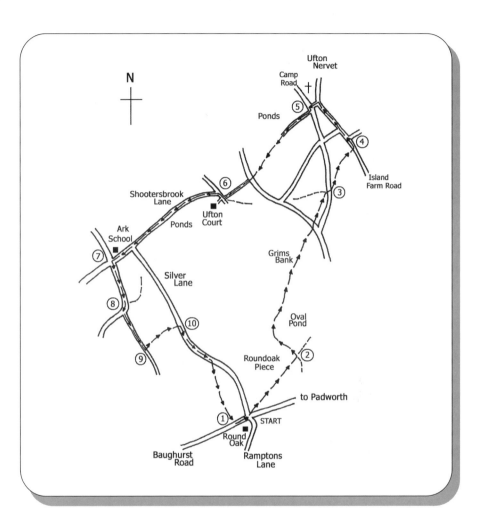

Introduction

This interesting walk starts at Padworth Common, a favourite haunt of highwaymen and footpads during the stagecoach era. The first part takes you through woodland as it heads for the village of Ufton Nervet. From here the route heads west towards Padworth, passing Ufton Court, a 15th-century Tudor manor house, which has some medieval fishponds in its grounds. Fine views across the Kennet valley can be seen before the route turns south to return to Padworth Common.

Drive and Stroll

The Round Oak

This pleasant inn serves London Pride, Thatcher's Gold and John Smith's beers, which you can imbibe whilst deciding what to eat from a varied menu, including baguettes, bangers and mash, salads, or something more substantial from the specials board. Food is served between 12 noon and 2 pm daily, and between 6 pm and 9 pm, except Sundays. Telephone: 0118 970 0365.

THE WALK

Leave the inn car park and turn right along the road. At the crossroads, turn left across the road, then right across a single-track lane to a barrier on the corner opposite. Pass the barrier and follow a wide track through woodland, known as **Roundoak Piece**.

At a wide cross track, turn left. At the next track junction, turn right, remaining on the gravelled track. The track soon starts to descend and passes a small pond **(Oval Pond)**, on the right. Beyond the pond, the track ascends again and meanders left and right. To your left you will soon see a small bank. This is **Grim's Bank**.

Although the origins of Grim's Bank are obscure, it is thought that the inhabitants of Silchester built it as a defence against the Saxons who were advancing up the Thames. The word Grim is a nickname for Woden and thus associated with evil and the Devil. Parts of the bank are visible at various points along this walk.

Continue along the track until you reach a road. Cross the road, with care, and follow a meandering path through the trees on the opposite side. Grim's Bank is still visible on your left. At the far side, the path runs parallel with a road until it reaches a footpath sign.

Turn right, through a gap, and cross the road. Pass a barrier on the opposite side and continue along an enclosed path, following a line of telegraph posts, until you reach another road.

Turn left along **Island Farm Road** and, ignoring turns to the right and left, follow it until you reach a road junction, with Ufton Nervet parish church just opposite. Turn left, keeping the church on your right. At the next road junction, turn left along **Camp Road**. In 50 yards, look for a footpath sign on the right.

View over the Kennet valley

Turn right here, pass a barrier, along an enclosed track. At the far end, cross a stile beside a gate and continue ahead along the left-hand edge of a field. Go over another stile and along the edge of a small wood to reach a minor road. The thatched Ufton Court Lodge is on your left. Cross the road and go down the main drive opposite leading to **Ufton Court**.

Ufton Court is a fine example of a Tudor manor house. Its 6.5 hectares of grounds include areas of lawn, an orchard, a 16th-century tithe barn and medieval fishponds. Just before the barn, on the left, there is a solitary fenced evergreen tree, presented by W. R. Benyon to mark the Marvyn Dole from 1581 to 1981. During the 16th century, the lady of the house (Ufton Court) got lost in the woods. She was found by some local villagers and being so pleased she decided that, once a year, she would issue the local people with bread and flour. It was a tradition that was to last centuries and became known as the Marvyn Dole.

Where the drive divides, turn right for 50 yards and, at a footpath sign, turn left past a wooden barrier and down a shady track **(Shootersbrook Lane)**. The medieval fishponds, looking somewhat neglected, are on the left. Remain on the track, which starts to ascend, to reach a gate and farmyard **(Old Farm)**. Pass to the left of a barn to reach a road, at a bend. Continue straight ahead along **School Road**. Good views can be seen to the right. Pass the **Ark School**, on the right, to reach a crossroads.

 ⑦

Now turn left down a minor road. On reaching a sharp right-hand bend, ignore a footpath on the left and follow the road round the corner. As the road straightens out, look for a footpath on the left.

 ⑧

Turn left along a track, which is soon joined by a high wire fence on the left.

 ⑨

At a footpath junction, turn left. The wire fence will also be on the left but is now joined by our old friend, **Grim's Bank**. Some good sections of it can be seen. The path eventually emerges at a road.

 ⑩

Turn right along the road, down into a dip and up the other side. Just before reaching the top, look for a footpath on the right. Follow a faint path through the trees to a stile on the left. Go over this and bear slightly right across two fields. Maintain direction along the edge of the next field to reach a gate and stile. Go along a short drive, with houses on the left, to reach a road. **The Round Oak pub** is directly opposite.

Place of Interest Nearby

Calleva Roman town, although just over the border in Hampshire, is easily accessible from Padworth Common. At the crossroads, near the start of the walk, turn right and follow the minor roads to Silchester. Calleva was one of the most impressive Roman towns in the area; its surrounding walls of $1\frac{1}{2}$ miles enclosed an area of about 107 acres. Parts of the flint built walls can still be seen. To the north-east of the town there are the remains of an amphitheatre, which can also be visited.

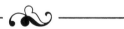

12 Upper Basildon

Thatched cottage at Stubbles

The Walk 5 miles ⏱ 3 hours
Map OS Explorer 159 – Reading, Wokingham & Pangbourne (GR 597761)

How to get there

This walk starts from the Red Lion public house in Upper Basildon. From the A340 in Pangbourne, take the road near the church signed to Upper Basildon. As you enter Upper Basildon, fork left to reach the Red Lion, which will be on the right. **Parking:** In the pub car park, but please seek the landlord's permission before leaving your car there while you walk.

Drive and Stroll

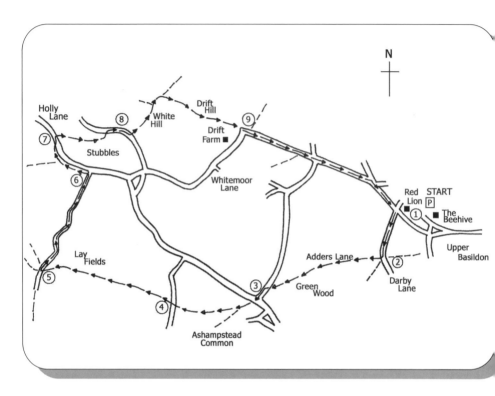

Introduction

This is probably the most strenuous walk in the book as it has a few ascents and descents. However, if you enjoy walking through woodland, then you will love this one. The route takes you through Green Wood and a wooded section of Ashampstead Common to the village of Stubbles and the outskirts of Ashampstead before returning, mainly by track and road, to Upper Basildon. Note that the shady woodland tracks can get quite muddy, even on the best of days so boots are essential.

The Red Lion

This is a popular village pub that serves food daily between 12 noon and 2.30 pm. It has a friendly relaxed atmosphere and the varied menu ranges from home-made pies and hot filled rolls, through to an à la carte selection. Sporting prints and pictures adorn the walls. Beers include Brakspear and West Berkshire ales. Telephone: 01491 671234.

THE WALK

With your back to the **Red Lion**, walk down the road opposite, signed to **Yattendon**. In approx 400 yards, where the road curves to the left, look for a track **(Adders Lane)** on the right.

Turn right and follow the track through trees and bushes. Adders Lane is quite shady and its condition, being used by farm vehicles, can get rather muddy at times. It is a pleasant track, however, which eventually drops down to emerge at a road.

Turn left to reach a road junction. Go straight across to the bridleway opposite. The path ascends quite steeply to wooded **Ashampstead Common**. Before you reach the top, have a rest and look back to see the countryside on the other side of the valley you have just crossed. At a footpath junction, ignore a yellow arrow pointing left, and continue straight ahead. The track runs just inside the edge of woodland, full of foxgloves in season. Where a track joins from the right, continue ahead to reach a road.

Cross the road, keeping just to the left of a house and garden. Pass through an open gateway and continue along a track that runs through more woodland **(Lay Fields)**. The track emerges from the trees and crosses an open area to reach a track junction. Bear right and, in 10 yards, you arrive at a stony cross track.

Turn right here and, ignoring a footpath going off to the left, remain on this stony track until you reach a road, at **Stubbles**. Note the attractive thatched cottage on your right.

Now turn left, using the path that runs inside the field just to the left of the road. At a gap, on the right, join the road and follow it round a sharp right-hand bend.

Near a telegraph post on the right, bear right onto a path that runs just to the right of a gate and paddock. At a footpath junction, turn right and follow a narrow path that meanders down through the trees and scrub to reach a road. Turn right along the road to reach, just after a right-hand bend, a minor road on the left.

Drive and Stroll

Turn left up **White Hill**. At the top, where the farm road bends to the right, continue straight ahead through more woodland. When the track emerges, you have an open field on your left. Stay on the track as it bends to the right, ignoring a path that crosses the field directly ahead. With woodland on the right, the track starts to ascend again and passes **Drift Farm**, on the right, before it merges with the farm drive. Continue along the drive to reach a road, at a bend.

The route now follows **Ashampstead Road** back to Upper Basildon. Continue straight ahead along the road, passing a small green at a road junction. At the first set of crossroads, keep straight ahead. At the next crossroads however, with **Maple Lane** opposite, turn right and follow the road down to return to the **Red Lion**, which will be on the left.

Places of Interest Nearby

Basildon Park is a National Trust property not far from the start of the walk. Surrounded by lawns and woodland, the 18th-century Palladian house has an unusual octagonal room. During the First World War it was used as a hospital. The popular writing paper known as Basildon Bond is named after the house and park. Entrance to the property is via the A329 Pangbourne to Streatley road. It is open between March and October. Telephone: 01494 755558.

Beale Park, in Lower Basildon, is an ideal place to take the children. Gilbert Beale, who died in 1967, created it for public pleasure under the Child Beale Trust. Among its many attractions are a miniature railway, a willow maze, a deer park and an assortment of interesting and exotic birds and animals. It is open daily between March and October. Telephone: 0118 984 5172.

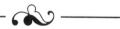

13 | Beenham

St Mary's church, Beenham

The Walk $4^3/_4$ miles 🕐 $2^1/_2$ hours
Map OS Explorer 159 – Reading, Wokingham & Pangbourne (GR 585688)

How to get there

From the M4 (junction 12), take the A4 towards Newbury. Before reaching the A340 roundabout, take a turning on the right, signposted to Beenham. Follow the road up through the village to reach the Six Bells public house, which will be on the right. **Parking:** At the Six Bells, with the landlord's permission. Alternative parking may be available at the Victory Hall, which is near Beenham primary school and before you reach the inn.

Drive and Stroll

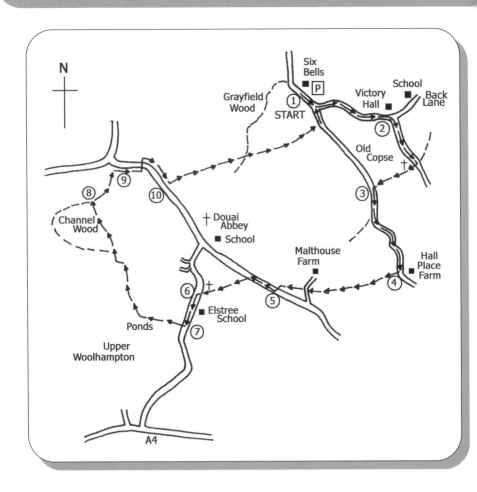

Introduction

Starting from the village of Beenham, this walk first takes you to Beenham church from where there are good views of the Kennet Valley. Field paths and tracks lead to Upper Woolhampton before the route turns north to Kiff Green. The return to Beenham passes close to Douai Abbey and school, which were established by Benedictine monks. A short detour off the route provides you with an opportunity to visit the abbey.

The Six Bells

Although improved and extended on a number of occasions, the building is thought to be over 200 years old. The inn has a beer garden and provides accommodation. A pleasant interior, with log fires in the colder months, invites you to sample the real ales on offer. Food varies from the staple English fare of cod and chips to lamb or pork chops with potatoes and vegetables. Note that the inn is closed at lunchtime on Mondays and Tuesdays. Telephone: 0118 971 3368.

THE WALK

With your back to the inn, turn left to walk through the village, bearing left at the junction along **Picklepythe Lane**. Pass the **Victory Hall** and the entrance to **Beenham primary school** on the left to reach a sharp left-hand bend.

Here, turn right across the road and head down the lane opposite, signed to Beenham church. At **St Mary's church**, turn right through the lych-gate. Keep to the left of the building to reach the main entrance. There are some good views to the south from here.

Inside St Mary's church a board informs you that the first vicar, in 1314, was Alexm de Quappelade. The current building dates from between 1859 and 1871. The bells were re-hung in a steel frame and were rung for the first time on 12 May 1937, the coronation year of George VI. The Archbishop of Canterbury (Robert Runcie) visited the church in 1988.

From the church entrance, bear left across the churchyard to reach a stile. Go over this and bear right across a field to reach a wood **(Old Copse)**. Follow a clear path through the wood, descending fairly steeply to cross a stone bridge at the bottom. Continue ahead to reach a stile and track.

Turn left down the track, ignoring a track and stile on the right. Keep to the main track as it bends right and left and ascends towards **Hall Place Farm**.

Just after passing a barn on the left, where the track bends left, turn sharp right to join a track that runs between fences at first. Where the fences end, continue ahead across a field towards the left-hand corner of a copse. Go through a gap and, with the copse on your right,

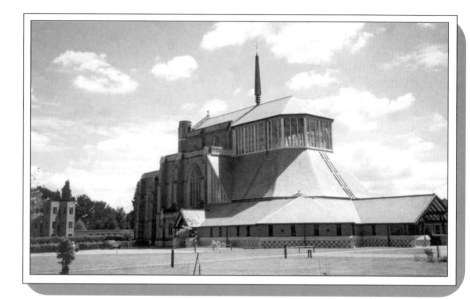

continue along the field edge. At the far corner, cross a stile and follow a meandering path through **Gravelpit Copse** to reach a path junction at the far side. Go straight ahead, through a very narrow squeeze stile. Bear slightly left across four fields, including a farm track, to reach a stile and road.

Turn right and, in 30 yards, just after a gate, bear left through some trees. Go straight over a drive, through a gap, and bear left along the field edge. Just before reaching the far corner, veer right to go through a gate and into the churchyard of **St Peter's church, Woolhampton**. Pass to the left of the flint-walled church to reach a road.

The 13th-century church of St Peter (rebuilt in 1861) includes a stained-glass window made by Thomas Williment, who was a heraldic artist for George IV and Queen Victoria.

Turn left along the road, passing **Elstree school** on the left and, 50 yards beyond the main entrance, look for a kissing gate on the right.

Turn right, through the gate, and follow a grassy track downhill, passing to the right of some small ponds. After a right-hand bend, go straight over a farm track and continue ahead on a narrower path. Go over two stiles and, at a footpath sign, bear right along the edge of a field. Bend left at the field corner and, in 40 yards, turn right over a stile. Follow a meandering path through **Channel Wood** to reach a footpath junction. Bear right along a track. At the next junction, turn right into a field and immediately turn left up the field edge, with the wood now on your left.

 ⑧

At the top corner, turn right. **Douai Abbey** can be seen from here, ahead and to the right. At the next corner, turn left to reach a road, at **Kiff Green**.

 ⑨

Turn right along the road. In 100 yards there is an option to use field paths that run parallel with the road, first on the right, then on the left. Although the road is not busy, it is narrow and there are no verges. Continue, either by road or path, until you reach a track on the left. (If you wish to visit **Douai Abbey** continue along the road for about 400 yards, then return to this point.)

Seeing the magnificent church at Douai Abbey it is almost difficult to believe that building work started in the 1920s. It was left unfinished until the Benedictine community decided to complete the work in 1993. Stained-glass windows were added by Henry Haig in 1999. The Benedictine monks, from Douai in northern France, came to Woolhampton in 1903. A pastoral programme of retreats, concerts and conferences are organised throughout the year.

 ⑩

Turn left along the track (turn right if you have been to the Abbey). When the track ends continue along the edge of a field. At the far corner, at a footpath sign, continue straight ahead just inside the edge of a wood. At the far side, pass a metal barrier, and continue towards Beenham. On reaching a track, turn left. At **Jayswood Cottage**, turn right to reach **Picklepythe Road**. Turn left to return to the **Six Bells**, or right to return to the **Victory Hall**.

Place of Interest Nearby

The Kennet and Avon Canal Visitor Centre, Aldermaston Wharf, just off the A340, is usually open between 1st April and 31st October. The Centre provides refreshments, souvenirs and information about the canal, boat trips, and other British waterways. Admission is free. Telephone: 0118 971 2868.

14 Brimpton and Wasing Park

The Walk 5 miles 🕒 3 hours
Map OS Explorer 159 – Reading, Wokingham & Pangbourne (GR 567628)

How to get there

From the A4, at Lower Padworth, take the A340 through Aldermaston towards Basingstoke. At Heath End, leave the A340 and turn right along the B3051 for just over a mile. The Pineapple public house will be on the left. **Parking:** There is limited parking available in a lay-by opposite the inn.

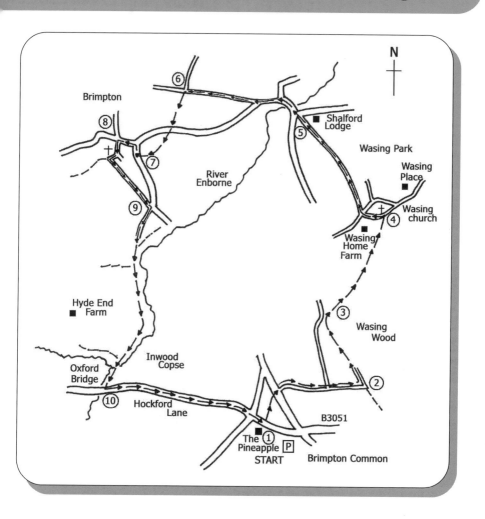

Introduction

This walk starts from the Pineapple in Brimpton Common. Here, the B3051 road forms the boundary between Berkshire and Hampshire. The inn, being on the south side of the road, is in Hampshire. The walk, however, is almost entirely in Berkshire. Leaving Brimpton Common the route takes you along the edge of Wasing Wood, through Wasing Park, and on to the village of Brimpton before returning, via field paths, to Brimpton Common.

Drive and Stroll

The Pineapple

This charming inn is very popular and tends to get busy on most days. The site on which the pub stands is mentioned in the Domesday Book. The current building, however, dates from about 1550. The pineapple after which it is named, is thought to relate to the pine cone, or 'pine apple', rather than the fruit. Food available includes sandwiches, jacket potatoes and more substantial fare. Beers include Flowers, Abbot Ale and Adnams. Telephone: 0118 981 4376.

THE WALK

①

With your back to the inn, cross the road to a path on the opposite side. Follow this enclosed path, over two stiles, to reach a road. Cross the road and continue along a private track **(Brimpton Lane)** opposite. Remain on the track until you reach a path/track junction at the far end. Continue straight ahead, passing a cottage, on the left, called **Wasing Wood Edge**. At **Woodside** cottage, pass between some short wooden posts and enter the wood, joining a path coming in from the right.

②

Turn left. Just before reaching a wider track, turn left through a gap in the hedge and immediately turn right along the field edge. Where the field hedge bends to the right, go directly ahead across the field. At the far side, go over a footbridge and continue on a narrow path

through a corner of **Wasing Wood** to reach a wider track, at a T-junction.

③

Turn right here and follow the track as it runs along the edge of the wood. Pass **West Lodge**, on the left, and in 20 yards, turn right around a metalled gate. In a further 30 yards, at a T-junction, turn left. Go through a swing gate at the far end, over a farm track, and through the swing gate opposite. Head across the field **(Wasing Park)** aiming just to the left of **St Nicholas's church**. At the far side, go though another gate to reach a drive.

St Nicholas's church, Wasing, was rebuilt in 1761 although parts of the building date back to the 15th century. The church is very long and narrow and, in its earlier days, is thought to have had some connections with the Knights Hospitallers, a religious order during the Middle Ages. On the churchyard gates can be found the dates of Sir William Mount and his wife. Wasing Place, seen to the right of the church, was originally built during

the 1770s. It burnt down during the Second World War and was rebuilt using some of the original stone.

Turn left along the drive, through a gate, to reach a junction. Bear right, then left along the drive heading downhill. Remain on the drive until you reach the Lodge at the bottom. Go through the gates and out to a road.

Turn left. At the road junction, turn right over a bridge spanning the **River Enborne**. Follow the road as it bends left and, at the next junction, bear left (signed to **Brimpton**). When the road bends sharp left, continue straight ahead through a swing gate. With Shalford Lakes on the right, carry straight on along a track, and then along the left-hand edge of a field.

Where a track joins from the right, turn left along an enclosed path to reach a road. Turn right and in 30 yards, at a footpath sign, turn left up a bank, through a gate and up the left-hand edge of a field. At the top corner, go through a gate on the left and along the edge of the next field. In 30 yards, turn right between houses to reach a road. Bear left up the road opposite to reach a T-junction. Cross the road to the archway opposite.

The archway leads to St Peter's Almshouses. Words engraved on the archway inform you that the Countess of Falmouth founded these in 1854. Seven almshouses were built to provide accommodation for aged couples and widows. Today, they have been converted into flats.

Drive and Stroll

 ⑦

Turn right along the road, passing Hatch Lane on the left. At the next road junction, with the **Three Horseshoes pub** on the corner, follow the road around as it bends left.

 ⑧

In 100 yards turn left, past the war memorial, to reach the lychgate of **St Peter's church**. Take the path that runs to the left of the church, following it round to reach a field. Turn left and follow the path downhill to reach a gate at the bottom, near a road.

 ⑨

Go through the gate and immediately turn right through another gate. Follow the track, first with a hedge on the right, then on the left. Soon you will see the **River Enborne** coming into view on the left. Ignore the first footbridge on the left. Some 25 yards beyond this, however, turn left, to cross over a second footbridge. Now walk directly across a field, heading towards some woodland. On reaching the river, turn right.

Keeping the meandering river on your left, follow a faint path across a few fields to reach a footbridge and footpath junction. Across the fields to your right the buildings of Hyde End can be seen.

The Hyde family, who lived at Hyde End House from the 16th to the 18th century, gave the settlement its name. Anne Hyde, the wife of James II is thought to have lived there for a short time. During the Second World War the house was used as the headquarters of the Great Western Railway.

Cross the bridge and follow a narrow path through woodland to reach a road.

 ⑩

Turn left along the road, ascending gradually. You are now walking along the border between Berkshire, on your left, and Hampshire, on your right. At the top, stop and turn to look at the view behind. At a road junction, go straight across, keeping to the left of a grassy central triangle, to return to the **Pineapple**, which will be on your right.

Place of Interest Nearby

The Vyne, at Sherborne St John, is within easy reach of Brimpton Common. The house was built in the 16th century for Lord Sandys, Henry VIII's Lord Chamberlain. It contains a fascinating Tudor chapel and a Palladian staircase. There are also attractive grounds to walk around and there is a shop and restaurant. The property is now owned by the National Trust. Telephone: 01256 881337.

15 | Hampstead Norreys

On the path near Banterwick Farm

The Walk 5 miles ⏲ 3 hours
Map OS Explorer 158 – Newbury & Hungerford (GR 531763)

How to get there

From Newbury follow the B4009 towards Streatley. As you drive through the village of Hampstead Norreys, the White Hart public house, where the walks starts, is on the left just before a sharp right-hand bend.
Parking: If you park in the pub car park, please seek permission before leaving your car whilst you walk.

Drive and Stroll

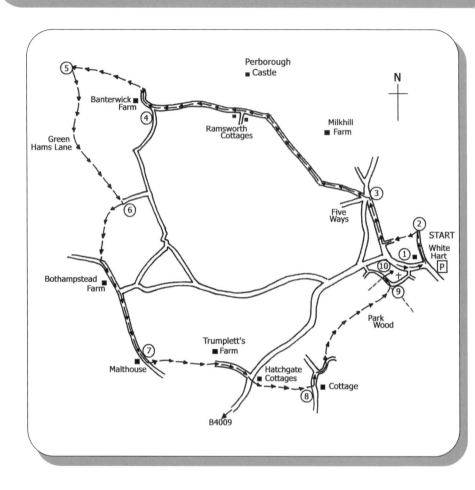

Introduction

This pleasant walk in the Berkshire Downs area provides some fine views of the rolling countryside. There are a few short ascents and descents but nothing strenuous. The village, mentioned in the Domesday Book, had many names up until 1450 when it took on its current title – Hampstead Norreys. Look out for an interesting tomb and the village well near the end of the walk.

The White Hart

Dating back to the 18th century, this is now the only inn in the village. Inside, the bar is quite spacious and there is a good-sized dining area. Fairly low wooden beams add to the atmosphere of the inn. At the rear there is a terrace and small garden. Food, which is available daily, ranges from snacks to more substantial offerings which you can select from a display board. Telephone: 01635 202248.

THE WALK

Leave the car park and turn left. Pass the front of the inn and immediately turn left along a track. Keep to the right of some farm buildings and continue ahead for 100 yards to reach a cross path.

Turn left across a field, towards some houses, keeping just to the left of a mid-field telegraph post. At the far side, go along a drive to reach **Water Street**. Turn right and follow the road until you reach a junction, with a house called **Five Ways** on the left.

Turn left before a grassy triangle, passing the front of the house. Cross the road, diagonally left, and continue along the track opposite. In 20 yards, fork right up the gently ascending track. Just beyond the top, as the track begins to descend, **Milkhill Farm** can be seen in the valley to your right. At the bottom the track bends left and you soon reach **Ramsworth Cottages**. On the hill to your right is **Perborough Castle**, the site of an Iron Age fort. Pass to the right of the cottages and continue along the track towards **Banterwick Farm**. Ignore a track on the left, just before reaching the farm.

Follow the track round as it bends to the right, passing the farmhouse and a barn. Some 50 yards beyond the barn, just before an entrance into a field, turn left and follow the track that runs along the field edge, with a hedge on your right.

At the far end, go through a gap and turn left at a cross track. At first the track **(Green Hams Lane)** runs through an avenue of trees and bushes before emerging through an open area to reach a field. Continue along the left-hand edge of the field to reach a cross track.

Turn right and follow the track, which bends left, until you arrive at

a road. Bear left along the road, passing **Bothampstead Farm**, on your right. Pass a road on the left, signed to **Hampstead Norreys**, and continue towards **Hermitage**. Pass **Malthouse**, on your right, and in 50 yards look for a bridleway sign on your left.

Turn left here, crossing the field towards **Trumplett's Farm**. Pass to the right of a barn and cross the farmyard to reach a lane. Bear right and follow the road down to reach a junction, with **Hatchgate Cottages** just opposite. Bear right across the road and take the path just to the right of the cottages. The path crosses a disused railway and then bears left up the left-hand edge of a field. At the far side go through a gap and continue ahead, now with a small wood on your right. Some 40 yards before reaching the far corner, turn right to emerge at a road, with **Cling Hill Cottage** just opposite.

Turn left down the road. In 100 yards, turn right up a wide track. At a track junction, fork left into **Park Wood**, which is part of the Eling estate. Follow the track through the wood and at the far side, bear slightly left, ignoring a path going left and a track on the right. Continue ahead, passing young trees growing on your right, before re-entering the wood. In 40 yards you reach a cross track.

Turn left downhill to reach a path junction. Turn left, soon with a graveyard on your left. Read the noticeboard near the entrance. This informs you a little bit about **Hampstead Norreys Motte**, of which very little is known. At the entrance, turn right to reach a footpath junction. Go straight across into the churchyard and head towards

St Mary's church. On the right side of the church is the **Lowsley Tomb**.

The Lowsley family tomb takes the form of a stepped pyramid. It was created in 1855 entirely from farm implements that were melted down and re-structured to form the pyramid.

Go through the church gates and turn right along the road, passing the village well on your left.

The well, enclosed by wooden paling, is one of the few remaining in Berkshire. It is no longer in regular use, but the machinery for raising water is still intact. Harry Weber presented it to the village 1903.

The White Hart public house is a short distance along the road, on the left.

Place of Interest Nearby

The Living Rainforest, Hampstead Norreys, provides the visitor with an opportunity to experience the sights, sounds and smells of a tropical rainforest. It was established in 1991 on the site of an orchid nursery. With accessible paths, gift shop, café and picnic facilities it has something for everyone. Telephone: 01635 202444.

16 Thatcham and Greenham Common

The Walk $5^1/_4$ miles ⏱ 3 hours
Map OS Explorer 158 – Newbury & Hungerford (GR 506670)

How to get there

From Newbury, take the A4 towards Reading. After passing the B3421 junction, signed to Newbury racecourse, take the next road on the right (Lower Way). Follow this towards Thatcham and look for a turning on the right leading to Thatcham Reedbed Nature Reserve. **Parking:** There is ample free parking at the nature reserve near the Discovery Centre from where the walk begins.

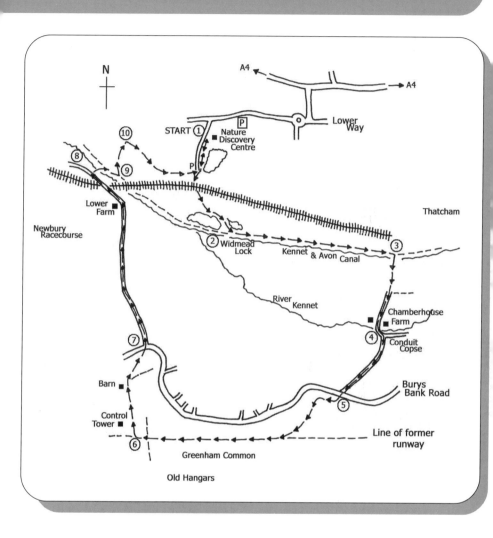

Introduction

Thatcham Nature Reserve, in addition to reedbeds, has lakes, moist woodland, a river and a canal, all forming a varied wetland landscape. It is an area attractive to wildlife. Greenham Common was notorious for the anti-nuclear demonstrations that took place there during the last two decades of the 20th century. The cruise missiles have now gone and the common has returned to natural heathland containing a wide range of wild plants and flowers. This fascinating nature walk visits both sites.

Drive and Stroll

Thatcham Nature Discovery Centre

The Centre was opened in 1995, by Newbury District Council, to provide information and education for school children and the local community. It has a gift shop, hands-on exhibitions and a small café. For opening times, telephone: 01635 874381.

THE WALK

Facing the Discovery Centre, turn right and take the path that runs alongside **Thatcham Lake**, which will then be on your left.

The island in the middle of the lake has a sand martin bank. Moorhen, mallard, coot and the great crested grebe may also be seen nesting around the lake.

Where the path bends left, go straight ahead between barriers. Continue along a track passing a small car park on your right to reach the Reading-Newbury railway line. Cross this with care and go through the barrier opposite. Now follow an enclosed path, passing a fishing lake on the right, to reach the **Kennet and Avon Canal**.

Turn left along the towpath, passing **Widmead Lock**, until you reach a swing-bridge.

Turn right over the canal and continue along a track, passing a mast on your right. Carry straight on to pass between the buildings of **Chamberhouse Farm**. Remain on the track, now metalled, as it passes over the **River Kennet** and bends to the left.

Just after the bend, turn right up a track taking you through **Conduit Copse** and on to reach a road **(Burys Bank Road)**. Cross with care and go through the gate opposite onto **Greenham Common**.

Greenham Common was taken over by the Air Ministry in 1941. It later became a base for the American Air Force and the first cruise missiles arrived in 1981. It is now a Site of Special Scientific Interest (SSSI) and is home to many rare and endangered plants. As such, walkers are requested to keep to the paths.

Turn right and follow the path that runs parallel with the road. On the horizon to your left, you may be able to see the top of **Watership Down**. Remain on the path as it bends left and, at a junction, bear right between some small trees. In a short distance a wider track joins from the left. Bear right here. This track was once the northern taxiway. When you are parallel with the old hangars on your left, branch right and head towards the old **Control Tower**. Go over a cross track, past a hewn log-seat, and continue ahead for about 50 yards.

Now turn right. Pass to the right of the **Control Tower** and head towards a barn. Pass to the right of the barn, following a grassy track. Just after a right-hand bend, turn left along a faint track. Twenty yards after this bends to the right, turn left through a gap to reach the boundary fence. Turn right to reach a gate on the left. Go through the gate, down a bank to a road. Cross, with great care, to the track opposite.

Follow the track down through **Bowdown Woods Nature Reserve** and continue ahead to pass **Bowdown Farm**, on the left and **Lower Farm Quarry** on the right. Keep straight ahead, past **Lower Farm**, and remain on the track, now more of a road, as it bends left and passes under the railway. Remain on the road until you reach **Clear Wise**, at the start of a business estate, on the left.

Here, turn right to cross a bridge over the **Kennet and Avon Canal.** Turn right along the footpath, with the canal on your right, to reach a bridge over the **River Kennet**.

Immediately after crossing this bridge, turn left along a path that meanders through the **Nature Reserve Reedbeds** passing over two small streams.

After crossing the second stream, turn right along a permitted path, soon with a wire fence on your left. On reaching a track, at a bend, continue straight ahead to go through a small parking area. At a track junction, bear left across the track and go through the barrier opposite. Now turn left, with **Thatcham Lake** on your right, and follow the path back to the Discovery Centre.

Place of Interest Nearby

Visit the **West Berkshire Museum** at the Wharf in Newbury and read the history of Greenham Common or see some archaeological artefacts that have been found in the area. Telephone: 01635 30511.

17 | East Ilsley

The Walk 3³/₄ miles 🕐 2 hours
Map OS Explorer 158 – Newbury & Hungerford (GR 493812)

How to get there

Leave the M4 at junction 13 and take the A34 towards Oxford. In 5¹/₂ miles look for a turning on the left, signed to East Ilsley. The road loops back under the A34 and as you enter the village the Swan public house will be on the right. **Parking:** In the pub car park but please seek permission before leaving your car whilst you walk. Alternatively, there is some limited roadside parking nearby.

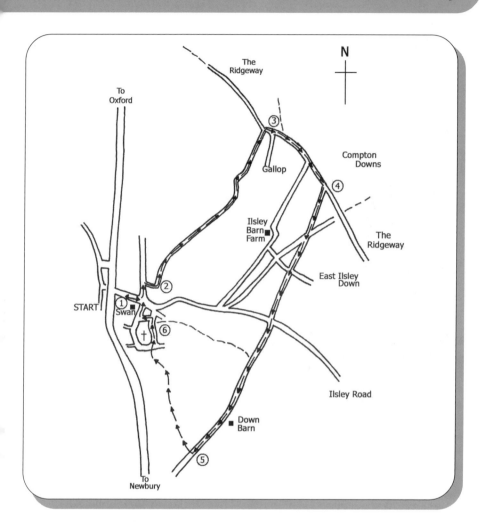

Introduction

This short, but pleasant, walk starts from the once well-known sheep market village of East Ilsley, or Market Ilsley as it was called. The route gently ascends the Berkshire Downs to meet up with the Ridgeway. From here there are some excellent views of the south Oxfordshire countryside. The towers of Didcot power station are also visible. Leaving the Ridgeway, the walk takes a semi-circular route to the west before returning to the village.

Drive and Stroll

The Swan Inn

Built during the 16th century, this one-time coaching inn is spacious and neatly decorated. It has a pleasant informal atmosphere and the traditional pub fare includes cod and chips, pies and interesting vegetarian dishes. Beers served include Greene King, Abbot Ale and IPA. It has an enclosed terraced garden and a small play area. Telephone: 01635 281238.

THE WALK

Leave the inn car park and cross the road, diagonally right, to **Abingdon Road** opposite. Walk along this 'No Through Road', passing **Farriers Lane**, on the right, until you reach **Sheepdown**, a road on your left. Turn right here, up a drive. This soon becomes a path and reaches a path junction.

Turn left up a bridleway, passing a tennis court, on your right. The path runs between hedgerows at first, then along the left-hand edge of a field. On the hillside to your right you can see **Ilsley Barn Farm**. As you continue to ascend, views of the rolling Berkshire Downs begin to open out. At the top, go straight over a gallop, to reach a wide cross track – **the Ridgeway**.

The Ridgeway is considered to be one of the oldest tracks in England. It existed as a highway long before the Romans arrived in Britain. It is now an officially designated National Trail that stretches for about 85 miles between Avebury, in Wiltshire, to Ivinghoe Beacon, in Buckinghamshire. Although the ancient track extend runs along the ridge of the Downs, when the Vale of the White Horse district was transferred to Oxfordshire in 1974, very little was left in Berkshire.

Turn right along the **Ridgeway**. Go straight over the first cross track. Looking to your left you should now have some good views towards Oxfordshire, including the cooling towers of Didcot power station slightly behind you. Just before reaching a small copse on the right, just to the right of the farm track leading to **Ilsley Barn Farm**, there is a water tap and a trough. The tap was not working when I passed by. Beside the trough there is a memorial stone.

The memorial stone has been placed there in memory of a Dr Basil Phillips LVO, who was a GP in the Newbury area. The words on the stone reveal that 'He was a countryman'.

Continue along the Ridgeway until you reach the next cross track.

④

Now, turn right along a track that runs between fences. Go straight over a cross track and continue to descend until you reach a road. **East Ilsley** is visible over to your right. Cross the road, with care, and carry on along the track opposite. Unless you want to make a quick return to **East Ilsley** ignore a path on your right and continue to ascend along the main track. Beyond a barn, on your left, you arrive at a staggered cross path.

 ⑤

Turn right down a path that runs between fields, keeping to the right of a hedge where it exists. As you drop into a dip, the village of **East Ilsley**, which you had been heading towards, completely disappears. It is almost like a David Copperfield illusion. As you near the village, the path bends left, then right, past a playing field before emerging at a road. Continue ahead down the road, passing a school and St Mary's church on the left, to reach a road junction.

 ⑥

Turn left, passing a post-box and bus shelter. At the next road junction, turn right. Look out for a memorial stone on a grassy bank on the right as you walk down the road.

A plaque on the memorial stone commemorates the history of East Ilsley from the day, during the 13th century, when it received a Royal Charter, through to the 17th century when it held a most important sheep fair, second only to that of Smithfield in London. The last sheep fair to be held in the village was in 1934. Today, the village, together with its neighbour West Ilsley, is more noted for its racing stables.

Continuing down the road you soon arrive back at the Swan public house, which will be on your left. On your right is another inn, the Crown and Horns, which was used as the setting for the 'Dog and Gun' in a BBC serial called *Trainer*.

Place of Interest Nearby

Didcot Rail Centre recreates the golden age of steam, with particular reference to the Great Western Railway (God's Wonderful Railway). Here, one can see a number of restored steam locomotives, a country station and a signal box. There is also a small museum to visit. For details and information, telephone: 01235 817200.

18 Kintbury

The Walk 6 miles 🕐 3$\frac{1}{2}$ hours
Map OS Explorer 158 – Newbury & Hungerford (GR 386671)

How to get there

From the A4, between Newbury and Hungerford, take a turning south, signed to Kintbury. Go over the level crossing, near Kintbury station, and immediately turn right into the public car park (free).

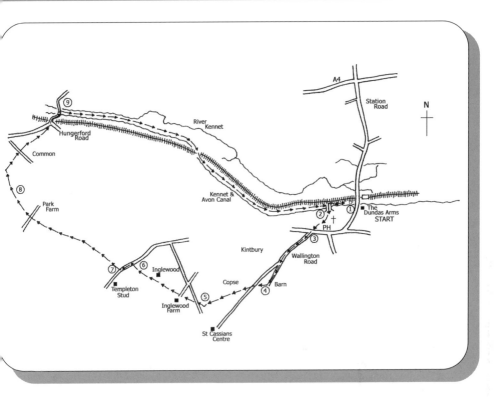

Introduction

Kintbury, as a settlement, dates back to Saxon times. At the time of the Domesday Book, the village was known as *Cynetanbyrig*. Agriculture was, and still is, the main industry in the area. This walk crosses some of this agricultural land as it heads south and west towards Hungerford. There are some good views looking south towards Walbury Hill and Inkpen Beacon. After crossing a section of Hungerford Common, the return to Kintbury follows the towpath of the Kennet and Avon Canal.

The Dundas Arms

The inn, which is named after Charles Dundas, the first chairman of the Kennet and Avon Company, occupies a prime position on the southern bank of the Kennet and Avon Canal. Inside there is a main bar, family room and a restaurant. Food is available daily except on Sunday and Monday evenings. Telephone: 01488 658263.

83

Drive and Stroll

THE WALK

Leave the car park through any of a number of gaps in the hedge to reach the canal towpath. Turn right for 300 yards to reach a bridge over the canal.

Bear right up the slope and turn left over the canal and head towards **Kintbury church**. Go up some steps and, at the top, continue straight ahead through the churchyard, keeping the church on your left.

The tower and Norman doorway of St Mary's church date from the 12th century but most of the other features of the church have been modified and altered. Inside there are a number of memorials to the Dunn, Shaw and Blandy families, all ancestral owners of the manor of Inglewood.

Leave the churchyard via the gate in the far right-hand corner and veer right along an enclosed path. At the far end turn left to reach a road, with the **Blue Ball pub** on your left.

In 1830 Kintbury was the scene of a riot led by a group of farm labourers who were concerned about the increasing mechanisation that was taking place on their farms. A detachment of Grenadier Guards arrived from London to quell the riot. Approximately 100 arrests were made. It is reported that most of the labourers were found in the Blue Ball public house.

Turn right for 30 yards. At the road junction, turn left along **Wallington Road** (signed to St Cassian's Centre). Where the road bends right into the grounds of **St Cassian's**, continue straight ahead along a grassy track, passing a lodge, on your right. On reaching a barn, bear right up the bank to reach a marker post at the field edge.

Turn right across the field. Go over a drive and stile, and bear slightly left across the next field. Pass just to the left of a small wood and maintain direction across the wild meadow. Go over a stile at the far side and continue ahead across the next field to reach a mid-field footpath junction. To your left you now have an excellent view of the **St Cassian's Centre**.

St Cassian's is a seminary for the De La Salle order. Between 1931 and 1975, when they moved to this centre, they were housed at Inglewood Manor.

At the footpath sign, turn right to reach a concrete track. Turn right

The Kennet and Avon Canal

and, in 50 yards, bear to the left of a gate to follow a path across a field, passing **Inglewood Farm**, on your left. Go over a drive and maintain direction across the next field. The buildings of **Inglewood** can be seen over to your right.

It is alleged that during the period that Henry VIII stayed at Inglewood, he used to meet Jane Seymour, who lived at Woolf Hall, just seven miles away. Inglewood is mentioned in the Domesday Book and has a long and interesting history.

Go through a gate in the far left-hand corner and turn right along the field edge. Go through another gate

and along a fenced path to reach a road.

Turn left along the road, passing the entrance to **Templeton Stud**, on your left. Continue ahead for another 150 yards to reach a footpath on the right.

The name 'Templeton' comes from the old manor that once belonged to the Knights Templar.

Turn right across a field. Go through a gap at the far side and turn right, then left, to follow the edge of a large field. Go over a track, leading to **Park Farm**, and continue along the edge of the next field. There are excellent views to your left looking towards Walbury Hill. Just before reaching the far corner bear right, through a gate, onto **Hungerford Common**.

Hungerford Common was the site chosen by General Eisenhower to address a reported 50,000 men prior to D-Day. From the Common it is just under $^1/_2$ mile to Hungerford station where you can catch a train back to Kintbury.

 ⑧

Pass to the left of a small copse then start swinging around in an arc, to

the right, across the common to reach a track. Keep to the left of the trees. Cross the track and then bear slightly right across another part of the common to reach a road. Turn right along the road (use the common) until you reach a road junction. Bear left here, over the railway, and follow the road round until you reach the **Kennet and Avon Canal**. The towpath is on the far side.

 ⑨

Turn right and follow the canal towpath, for a pleasant two miles, back to Kintbury. Just before **Kintbury Lock**, turn left into the car park.

Place of Interest Nearby

Hungerford, with its many antique shops, is a favourite haunt for the antique collector. Its historic Bear Hotel has played a major role as a meeting place for two major events in the history of this country. In 1688, William of Orange had a meeting with representatives, which ultimately led to James II fleeing to France. During the early 19th century (1810), a meeting was held at the same venue that led to the linking of the two canals that today form the Kennet and Avon Canal.

19 Wickham

The Five Bells at the start of the walk

The Walk 4 miles ⏲ 2 hours
Map OS Explorer 158 – Newbury & Hungerford (GR 395718)

How to get there

Leave the M4 at junction 14 and follow the A338 towards Wantage for just over half a mile. Then turn right along the B4000 **(Ermin Street)**, which passes back under the M4, to reach Wickham. As you enter the village, the Five Bells inn is on your left. **Parking:** At the inn or on street.

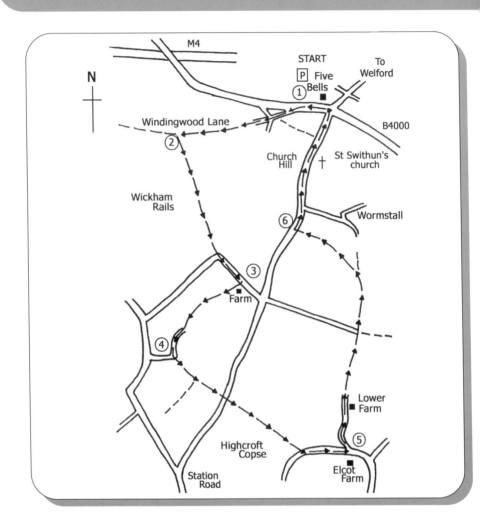

Introduction

This varied walk takes you across agricultural land to the south of the village, from where there are some excellent views looking south to the ridge and to the downs to the east of Walbury Hill. Using tracks and field paths, the route takes you to the settlements of Clapton and Elcot. Both contain nothing more than a farm and a few houses. The walk back to Wickham takes you pass St Swithun's church where, if you are lucky, you may see some elephants.

The Five Bells

This quaint thatched inn is over 400 years old. The bar area is attractive and cosy, with old wooden beams contrasting with the more modern brickwork. Its setting, close to racehorse training facilities in Wickham and other Berkshire Downs villages, tends to attract many customers who have connections with the racing fraternity. Food ranges from baguettes to Sunday roasts. Note, however, that food is not available on Sunday evenings. Telephone: 01488 657894.

THE WALK

With your back to the **Five Bells**, cross the road, with care, and turn right. In 150 yards, at a footpath sign, bear left along a track. Where this bends to the right, continue straight ahead along a hedge-lined path, which soon widens into a track **(Windingwood Lane)**.

The name Windingwood Lane has almost certainly earned its name from the fact that it once meandered through the extensive woodland that existed in this area.

In 400 yards you arrive a track junction, look out for the footpath sign.

Turn left along a bridleway that takes you through an area known as **Wickham Rails**. Remain on the track until it reaches a road, at a bend. Carry straight on along the lane for 200 yards where you will see some houses on the right.

Just before the houses, turn right through a gap and up the left-hand edge of a field. Keep to the field edge as it bends left, then right, passing **Orpenham Farm** on the left. At the top of the field go through a gap, passing a tennis court on the left, and continue along a track, with a small wood on your right. Where the track bends left, continue straight ahead, through a gap in the field corner, and along the edge of the next field. At the next corner, the path bends right, then left around the grounds of a house. The house is hidden behind a hedge. Beyond the house, the path joins the entrance drive, which is now followed. Just after a right-hand bend, look for a footpath sign on the left.

Turn left here between fields and keeping to the right of a hedge when this forms the boundary. There are some good views looking across to your right. Ignore a path going off to the right and continue

ahead, through a gap in the far corner, to reach a lane. Go straight across and maintain direction on the opposite side. Go through another gap and continue up the left-hand edge of a field. A new hedgerow has been planted on your left. Over to your right is the woodland of **Highcroft Copse**. At the top corner of the field continue ahead to reach a lane, with a house directly opposite. Turn left along the lane until you reach a junction, with **Elcot Farm** just ahead on the right.

 ⑤

Turn sharp left along another lane. Pass to the left of **Lower Farm** and

continue on to **Hill View House**, also on the right. Just beyond this property, the lane becomes a track. At a cross track, continue straight ahead. At a point where the track has become overgrown, turn right into a field and immediately turn left along the field edge. At the far corner, bear left along a track. In 50 yards, turn left through a gate and immediately turn right to go over a stile. Turn left along the field edge then through a small area of scrub. Go over two stiles and up the edge of the next field. **Wormstall**, a pony club centre, can be seen over to your right. Go over another stile and follow a path through some trees and scrub to reach a road.

Turn right, passing the entrance to **Wormstall**, and follow the road, ascending gradually. At the top of the hill you will see **St Swithun's church** on your right.

St Swithun's chapel/church, mentioned in the Domesday Book of 1087, stands on the site of an old Roman camp. The tower is considered to be one of the oldest in Berkshire, as it contains some Roman masonry. When the chapel was restored in 1845, the Rev. William Nicholson, who was vicar of Welford-cum-Wickham for 42 years until his death in 1878 at the age of 73, had intended to have angel figures erected at the ends of the hammer beams in the north aisle. However, during a visit to a Paris exhibition a few years later, he found some paper maché elephants and brought back four. An additional four were ordered and the eight elephants were duly set in place. Rev. Nicholson's body is interred in the burial ground at the east end of St Gregory's church in the grounds of Welford Park.

To complete the walk, continue ahead down the hill. At the crossroads, turn left to return to the **Five Bells**, which is over on your right.

Place of Interest Nearby

Welford Park and St Gregory's Church. A public footpath runs right through Welford Park to St Gregory's church in the grounds. St Gregory was Pope from AD 590 until his death in AD 604. In AD 596 he sent St Augustine to England on a Christian mission, and St Augustine went on to become the first Archbishop of Canterbury. Although there has been a church on the site for over 1,000 years, the current building dates from 1855.

Welford Park was built by renowned architect, Thomas Archer, in 1702. There had been a previous house on the site which had been used by Henry VIII as a hunting lodge. The house (which is not open to the public) is set in beautiful wooded parklands that are ablaze with masses of snowdrops, daffodils and bluebells in the spring. It is open to the public for certain days in February each year and is well worth a visit. Telephone: 01488 608691 for opening times.

20 | Lambourn

The Walk 5 miles ⏱ 3 hours
Map OS Explorer 158 – Newbury & Hungerford (GR 325788)

How to get there

Leave the M4 at junction 14 and take the A338 north. Take the first turn left (B4000) signed to Lambourn. **Parking:** As you approach the centre of the village, the car park is on the left.

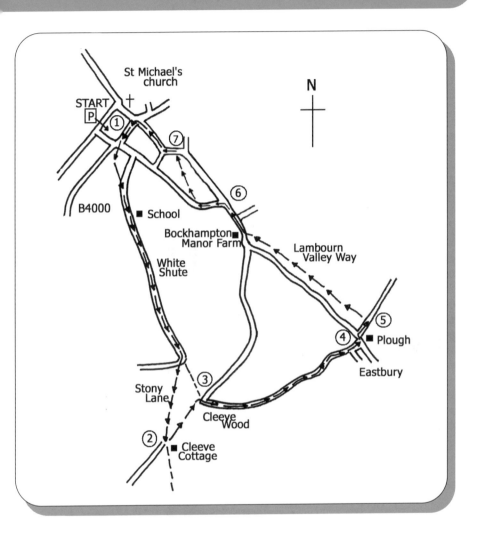

Introduction

This delightful walk, in the heart of the 'Valley of the Racehorse', follows paths and tracks to the south and west of the village en route to the village of Eastbury. Small and compact, with the River Lambourn flowing through it, Eastbury is well worth investigating and, as such, I suggest it as a good convenient lunch stop. The return to Lambourn is via the Lambourn Valley Way, which, for the most part, follows the line of a disused railway.

Drive and Stroll

The Plough, Eastbury

This pleasant inn, overlooking the River Lambourn, is thought to be over 250 years old. It is a favourite haunt of members of the racing fraternity, as well as walkers and cyclists who pass through the village. A good selection of bar meals is available, ranging from baguettes and jacket potatoes to chilli con carne or steak and Guinness pie. Booking is recommended at weekends. Telephone: 01488 71312.

THE WALK

Leave the car park and turn right up the **High Street**. At **Edwards Hill**, on the left, bear left up a fairly steep path. At the top, ignore a footpath on the right, and continue ahead along the road **(Greenways)**, passing **Lambourn C of E School**. At the entrance to **Meridan House**, ignore a bridleway on the right and continue ahead down a track **(White Shute)**. At the bottom, the track evens out before starting to ascend gradually between hedgerows. Remain on the main track, which soon starts to descend again, passing Watts Bank Nature Reserve, on the left.

Watts Bank Nature Reserve is situated on the site of an old quarry. Within its boundary, one can find a rich variety of wild flowers including, in season, the common spotted and fragrant orchids. Various varieties of birds and butterflies may also be seen.

Ignore all stiles leading into the reserve and continue along the path until you reach a junction, with a stile on your right and left. Ignore these and carry straight on to reach a junction of tracks, with **Cleeve Cottage** just ahead of you, to the left.

Turn sharp left, keeping the house and garden on your right. When the garden ends, you will have part of **Cleeve Wood** on your right. An open field soon appears to your left. At the far corner of the wood, you arrive at a path/track junction.

Turn right, keeping to the main track. The wood should still be on your right and soon you will have open fields on your left. Just after the wood ends, ignore a path going off to the left and continue straight ahead to reach a track junction. Bear left here. On a good clear day you should have some excellent views of the rolling countryside of the Berkshire Downs. The track starts to descend and eventually crosses the **River Lambourn** to emerge at the main road in

On the path near Lambourn

Eastbury. The **Plough Inn** is directly opposite.

Eastbury has links that date back to Norman times. A manor, on the western side of the village, has existed on the site since that period. The current manor dates from the early 15th century. The church of St James the Greater, not far from the inn, was designed by G.E. Street and built in 1851. It contains a memorial window, engraved by Laurence Whistler, to commemorate the lives of poet and writer, Edward Thomas and his wife Helen. He was a keen walker himself and some of his literary work contains good descriptions of the local countryside. In a small square opposite the church stands the Prayer Cross of St Antoline. Itinerant preachers and others once stood on the steps to preach to those who would stop and listen.

Turn left along the road. (Turn right if you have just come out of the inn.) In 30 yards, turn right. Pass **Montague House** on the left to reach a cross track.

Turn left here. You are now on the **Lambourn Valley Way**, which is followed all the way back to Lambourn. Just beyond

Drive and Stroll

Bockhampton Manor Farm, on the left, the path emerges onto a minor road. Turn left and within a few yards, turn right along the main road for 150 yards to reach a road junction.

Turn left down the road (signed to Bockhampton). Remain on the road as it bends to the right. The **River Lambourn** is now visible on your right. Just beyond a small corrugated-roofed barn and footpath on the left, bear right to go over a stile beside a six-bar gate. Cross a field and maintain direction across a sports field to reach a gate on the far side. Go through and continue ahead between houses. At a path junction carry straight on to reach a road.

Turn left, passing the 'Nippy Chippie' and 'Little India' and follow the road round as it bends to the right. It soon brings you to the crossroads in the centre of Lambourn, with **St Michael and All Angels church** directly opposite.

The nave of St Michael and All Angels church dates from the 12th century. Although changes have taken place over the centuries, many Norman features can be found in the church. Holy Trinity chapel, within the church, contains the tomb of John of Eastbury. In 1501 he founded the almshouses that can be seen to the north of the church. Henry Hippesley rebuilt the current almshouses in 1852. In the square near the church is the market cross; the original being erected when Henry VI granted a charter allowing Lambourn to hold a market and fairs. Lambourn's status as a centre for sheep markets changed in 1878 when William Jousiffe arrived from Newmarket. His setting up of a local training establishment was the start of the village's connection with the racehorse industry.

Turn left along the **High Street**. In 150 yards turn right to return to the car park.

Place of Interest Nearby

Ashdown House, near Lambourn, dates from the 17th century when the 1st Earl of Craven built it as a hunting lodge. Today, the Dutch-style house is more noted for its association with Elizabeth of Bohemia, sister of Charles I, to whom the house was 'consecrated'. The house and grounds, administered by the National Trust, are open on Wednesday and Saturday afternoons between April and October. Telephone: 01793 62209.